GLOUCESTER CATHEDRAL

Gloucester Cathedral

FAITH, ART AND ARCHITECTURE: 1000 YEARS

SCALA

CONTENTS

FOREWORD

THIS BOOK DESCRIBES a unique place with an extraordinary and rich history and exquisite architecture, containing some wonderful treasures. I hope it will bring back your own special memories of being in Gloucester Cathedral and encourage you to come back again and again, for it is a place that will reward you richly every time you visit.

The importance of the building for any occasional visitor or regular worshipper, or any volunteer for that matter, lies not in understanding the history, gazing in wonder at the stained glass or seeing the awe-inspiring cloisters for the first time, but in the experience of simply being in the timeless space the building encloses. Just being in the place is a wonderful experience. It makes me think of the countless men and women, kings and peasants, monks and masons, bishops and beggars, who have sung songs, carved stones, wondered and worshipped, thanked God for prayers answered or cried out to him in their grief in this place. Its purpose is the same as it has been for centuries, ever since it was built as a church for a Benedictine community in the eleventh century: to help ordinary men and women to experience more intensely the presence of God and bring them to their knees in prayer and – and more than that – to an understanding through the life, work, death and resurrection of Jesus Christ that they are loved by God and that love is as timeless as the building.

The building is an extraordinary survival, and this book describes how sometimes it has come close to being pulled down or been dreadfully neglected, but also how heroic efforts have been made to restore and conserve it. I am glad to say it is now in as good condition as it has ever been, though such a beautiful and delicate building will always need much energy and money spent on conservation and restoration because of the ravages of frost, wind and rain.

The great events in the history of England and the Christian religion have left their indelible marks. Kings and queens have worshipped here. One king was crowned here; another is buried here. Great musicians have made music, composed music and glorified God with their singing here. Stonemasons and architects have built or changed or restored the building through the centuries and made it more beautiful in their eyes. Abbots, bishops and deans have had new ideas and made great changes. Religious strife, civil war and great events have all left their mark. Some people have smashed up bits of it, treated it badly or wanted to do away with it altogether. Great men and women, brave soldiers and sailors, those who have changed our way of life for the better and those who have met tragedy, are all remembered here in wood and stone and glass. But for centuries ordinary people have also come – and still do come – as worshippers, pilgrims and visitors, said their prayers and encountered God in this place.

An ancient prayer, written by Benedict of Nursia in the sixth century, has been used by people visiting this place over the centuries. You too may like to use it:

O Gracious and Holy Father, give us wisdom to perceive you, diligence to seek you, patience to wait for you, eyes to behold you, a heart to meditate on you and a life to proclaim you; through the power of the Spirit of Jesus Christ our Lord. Amen

NICHOLAS BURY
Dean of Gloucester, 1997–2010

I THE BENEDICTINE INHERITANCE

FOUNDED IN THE ELEVENTH CENTURY, St Peter's Abbey in Gloucester became one of the great Benedictine monasteries of medieval England (fig. 1). The Rule of St Benedict was introduced here some time in the late tenth or early eleventh century and was followed for over 500 years until the abbey was dissolved by Henry VIII in 1540. Benedict of Nursia (480–c.547) wrote down his rule for monastic living towards the end of his life, in around 540, at Monte Cassino in central Italy. The Rule divided the day's activities into three: the *opus dei* (times of liturgical prayer), the *lectio divino* (spiritual reading and contemplation) and manual labour (tasks necessary to sustain the life of the community). The monks took vows of stability (meaning both staying in one place and living within the Rule), obedience and *conversatio morum* (ongoing conversion into disciples of Christ). Benedict wrote wise words about the qualities needed in an abbot, and he was concerned that every person in the community should have a voice in its deliberations. Hospitality was to be offered 'as if to Christ himself'. It was a way of life that proved to work well. However, St Benedict's Rule was not the only way of life for communities of monks and nuns. In Gloucester during the later Middle Ages there were several other orders. The Augustinians inhabited St Oswald's Priory and Llanthony Secunda, the Dominicans were at Blackfriars, and the Franciscans had a house at Greyfriars.

The Benedictine influence was strong in England after the Norman Conquest in 1066. Two post-conquest archbishops of Canterbury, Lanfranc and Anselm, had previously been abbots of the Benedictine abbey of Bec in Normandy. With its proximity to Wales and the trade route of the River Severn, Gloucester was an important strategic centre for William the Conqueror. St Peter's Abbey benefited from the royal influence and became more prominent when Serlo, possibly one of William's chaplains, was appointed abbot in 1072.

Over the next four centuries St Peter's Abbey, like many medieval monasteries, became a landowner on a scale that St Benedict could never have imagined. Gloucestershire was a centre for the wool trade, and the abbey became wealthy. With wealth came power. The abbot of St Peter's became a mitred abbot in the fourteenth century; this meant that he was a peer of the realm, with a role to play in the political life of the nation. The last abbot of Gloucester, Abbot Parker, spent much of his time in London, at the court of Henry VIII.

In addition to administering land and money, many abbeys were centres of learning and culture. Even when the universities began to flourish at Oxford and Cambridge in the thirteenth century, monasteries continued to educate the children of the nobility. A strong link with the Benedictines existed at both ancient universities. Gloucester College in Oxford was founded in 1283 with a gift from St Peter's Abbey; it became Worcester College only in 1714.

As the abbey was altered over the centuries from pure Romanesque to incorporate its Early English, Decorated and glorious Perpendicular elements, the medieval craftsmen gave England one of its greatest churches. Throughout those centuries the worshipping life of the Benedictine community continued. Week after week, year after year, the monks prayed and sang the eight daily offices in this abbey church built for the glory of God.

CELIA THOMSON

Fig. 1
Historiated initial 'Q' depicting Christ holding the cross of St Benedict, and Benedictine monks. Italian School, fifteenth century.

ABBOT SERLO AND THE NORMAN ABBEY

THE CATHEDRAL at Gloucester has been a centre of Christian worship for over 1,300 years. It originated in the late seventh century, during the earliest days of England, centuries after the Roman occupation, when a very different country was emerging under the control of Germanic immigrants. Regional kingdoms were forming whose rulers were accepting Christianity and building churches.

The Anglo-Saxon minster

In about 679 a monastery was founded in the derelict former Roman city of Gloucester. The patron was Osric, a ruler of the kingdom of the Hwicce. This kingdom covered a substantial part of the south-west Midlands; its bishopric, created at about the same time as the minster at Gloucester, was located at Worcester. By the late seventh century the kingdom of the Hwicce was already subordinate to the kings of Mercia, and by the end of the eighth century it had been absorbed into that kingdom.

Our knowledge of the early minster at Gloucester derives for the most part from materials written down many centuries later. However, it seems clear that at the time of its foundation Gloucester was a 'double minster' – that is, a house of both men and women ruled by an abbess. Double monasteries were favoured foundations of the aristocracy in Gaul and became popular in England also. The first three abbesses were called Cyneburg, Eadburg and Eafe, and all three were probably close relatives of the ruling family. Osric was buried in his foundation at Gloucester, as were the first three abbesses; other members of the family were probably also buried there.

These minsters were important stable establishments at a time when kings and their retinues were constantly on the move. The Gloucester minster acquired large estates and was almost a small town in itself, alive in the ruins of the Roman city. The place still had strategic importance – it stood on a major waterway, the River Severn, and on the crossing place of a main route into Wales.

Little is known of the minster during the second half of the eighth and the ninth century, though in 804 Gloucester received a major gift of land from a local magnate, Æthelric. By this time the Gloucester minster was no longer a nunnery but seems to have been a community of secular priests – not monks but men living under a regime that allowed the clerics to have individual households, and perhaps even wives. There is no information concerning the appearance of the minster; even its site is uncertain. We can imagine it as a complex of buildings with a richly decorated principal church. Only one remnant of the minster survives: part of a ninth-century screen with Christ depicted in a roundel on one face and a foliage design on the other (fig. 2).

From around 850 onwards Mercia was severely disrupted by Danish invasions, and the kingdom of Mercia collapsed in the course of the 870s. The minster community at Gloucester is likely to have

Fig. 2
Part of a ninth-century stone screen depicting the head of Christ. This is the only known remnant of the Anglo-Saxon abbey.

Fig. 3
Diagram by cathedral architect F. S. Waller, 1890, showing the surviving Romanesque church with all later additions removed.

suffered severely during a Danish occupation of the town in the first half of the winter of 877–78. Danish settlement was, on the whole, restricted to eastern Mercia, and from the 880s west Mercia was governed by Ealdorman Æthelred. Æthelred recognised the authority of King Alfred of Wessex (871–99) and married Alfred's daughter Æthelflæd. Together Æthelred and Æthelflæd restored and fortified Gloucester in the years around 900; an important assembly was held there in 896. The couple also introduced a rival establishment to the 'old minster': a New Minster, which was to receive relics of, and be named after, St Oswald of Northumbria. The ruins of the New Minster can still be seen today (see fig. 52).

The more ancient establishment was not eclipsed for long. In the late tenth or early eleventh century the old minster at Gloucester was reformed and became a regular monastery, with an abbot and monks living under the Rule of St Benedict. By then, the town of Gloucester was a growing urban centre and had become the administrative hub of the newly created shire of Gloucester. In the reign of King Edward the Confessor, Gloucester was one of the centres frequently visited by the king and his court. The royal palace of Kingsholm was half a mile north of the town, and here was held the 'crown-wearing', a coronation ritual repeated at the principal church festivals during the year at the three centres of Winchester, Westminster and Gloucester. In 1058 Ealdred, bishop of Worcester (1046–61), one of the leading diplomats of his day and later archbishop of York, refurbished the abbey at Gloucester, perhaps for the specific purpose of creating a grandiose setting for the crown-wearing. The ceremony was to be adopted by William I (1066–87), who also 'wore his crown' at Gloucester, usually at Christmas.

Fig. 4
The Norman crypt looking south-east, showing strengthened arches and pillars. The extra buttressing had to be added in the fourteenth century.

William conquered England against considerable odds; the conquered nation could be seen as having received divine judgement. Ambitious Norman churchmen were appointed to English positions. The new abbot at Gloucester, appointed in 1072, was Serlo, until then a monk at Mont St Michel in Normandy. Serlo found the monastery at Gloucester impoverished and reduced to two monks and eight boys. Under Serlo's guardianship, and with the financial support of Norman aristocrats, the number of monks was greatly increased, and new landed endowments were received. In 1095 even the estates that had been sequestered by Bishop (later Archbishop) Ealdred in Edward the Confessor's reign were returned to Gloucester Abbey.

In 1085 William and his court spent the Christmas season at Gloucester, assembling in the great hall at Kingsholm. Among other matters, the decision was taken to compile the great survey we know as Domesday Book, which catalogued 'what or how much everybody had who was occupying land in England'. The crown-wearing ceremony was also part of this occasion: it involved a procession from the Kingsholm chapel to St Peter's Abbey church, as rebuilt nearly thirty years earlier. The church was, however, near the end of its life. In 1088 it was badly damaged during warfare arising from opposition to William II (William Rufus, 1087–1100). The rebellion was put down, and plans were made to build a new church. The foundation stone was laid in 1089. The old church probably remained in use; it must have been used for crown-wearing ceremonies, which continued during the reign of William II. There were no more such ceremonies after 1100, and by then the new abbey church was sufficiently complete to be used for monastic worship. The Anglo-Saxon church was demolished.

The Norman abbey

Under Serlo's leadership Gloucester Abbey became famous; William of Malmesbury commented that Serlo was one of the three great abbots whose spirituality and rule over their abbeys distinguished them from all other ecclesiastics in England after the conquest, and Godfrey of Winchester noted in a poem that Serlo 'pleased the very princes whom he reproved'. Serlo died in March 1104, after more than thirty years as abbot. His achievement was to provide Gloucester Abbey with monumental architecture and an impressive monastic reputation.

The new church was in the architectural style often today known in England as 'Norman' but in

Fig. 5
The capital of one of the crypt pillars. Such moustaches were worn by Anglo-Saxon nobility at the time of the Norman Conquest.

Fig. 6
South ambulatory of the quire, looking east. Apart from the stone screens filling the arches, this view is much as it was in about 1100.

Normandy and France termed 'Romanesque'. The style imitated Roman buildings, using semicircular arches and gaining height and strength by the use of thick walls. A surprising amount of Serlo's church survives, although it is often disguised by later work (fig. 3). The crypt is largely as built in the late eleventh century, although the original design had to be strengthened as building work proceeded, by enlarging the pillars and inserting extra vault ribs (fig. 4). The crypt has an apsidal central chamber and a surrounding ambulatory, from which open five polygonal chapels. The central space is supported on twelve round columns topped with simple capitals, each slightly different. One of them carries a moustachioed face (fig. 5) similar to characters in the Bayeux Tapestry, which was made in the 1070s, probably in Canterbury, to celebrate the victory of William I at the Battle of Hastings.

The original purpose of a crypt was to contain relics and to facilitate processions of pilgrims. Therefore crypts had two entrances, one from each transept; the design had become part of the Romanesque tradition. At Gloucester the remnants of the northern entrance (blocked since the Middle Ages) can be seen on the north side of the crypt. We do not know what relics, if any, may have rested in the crypt.

Serlo's quire is reflected in the plan of the crypt beneath. It had a central apsidal space with a surrounding ambulatory and radiating chapels, including an eastern chapel; in the quire this has been superseded by the Lady Chapel, but it survives in the crypt below. The quire arches were set on low cylindrical piers (fig. 6), which, before the fourteenth-century alterations, continued in a semicircle behind the altar. Above the ambulatory and also imitating its plan, including the radiating chapels, was an arcaded gallery (fig. 7). Again, the

Fig. 8
The east side of the north transept. The round Norman openings can be seen behind the Perpendicular facing, though some of the openings have been converted to pointed arches.

gallery was part of the Romanesque tradition. It provided extra altars (chapels in the crypt, quire and gallery totalled fifteen), and its great quadrant arches (continuous built-in precursors of Gothic flying buttresses) served to support the walls and quire vault.

All the work in the eastern arm of the church was very plain, with simple cushion and scalloped capitals; some arches have no capitals at all. High up on the outside of the quire the stonework was decorated with a blind arcade. On the continent, especially in western and southern France, the quires of churches with this feature have a stone tunnel vault. If this was the case at Gloucester, then the quire would have been very dark, having perhaps three small high-level (clerestory) windows in the apse bays but otherwise illuminated only by borrowed light from the ambulatory and gallery. The quire was sunk down just over two feet lower than the

ambulatories; no one knows why, but we can be sure it was part of the original design because the same was done in the crypt.

The interior of the transepts was also very plain – each had a large arched opening into an eastern chapel and a smaller arch leading into the quire ambulatory (fig. 8). These pairs of arches were replicated at gallery level. In each transept is a stair turret, giving access to passages in the thickness of the wall at gallery, clerestory and roof level. Between the transepts, at the crossing, was a low tower with a circular turret at each corner. The scars of two of these turrets are visible in the nave roof space, and the base of one turret, reddened by the early twelfth-century fire, can still be seen on the exterior.

The south transept exterior was an exception to the theme of simplicity; it was embellished with blind arcading and plentiful chevron (zigzag) ornament. It was modified in the fourteenth century to receive

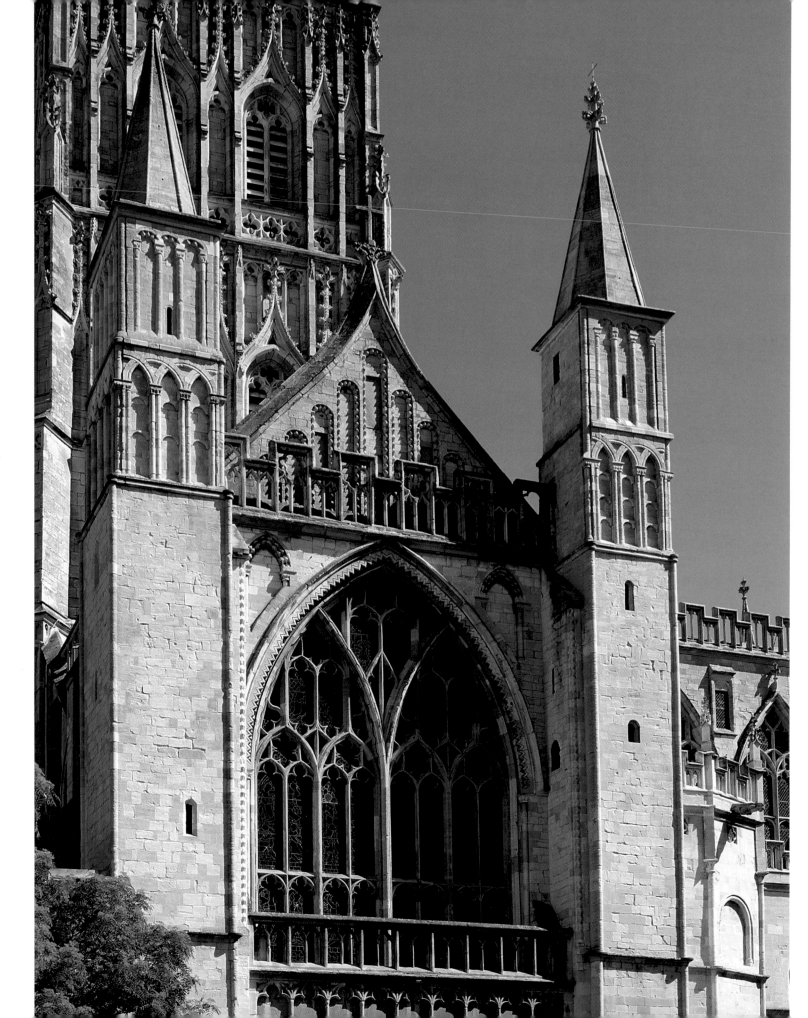

Fig. 10
Norman capitals in the nave north aisle. As the nave neared completion in the 1120s the decoration became more elaborate.

Fig. 9
Fourteenth-century masons put in a large new window in the south transept, but re-used Norman chevron and other decoration.

large windows, but the alteration reused the Norman decoration – so the outside elevation is fourteenth-century work with Norman detailing (fig. 9).

By the time the church was dedicated in 1100 the quire and transepts had probably been completed. After Serlo's death in 1104 the work continued. The nave was being built in the early twelfth century, though fires in 1101 and 1122 must have hindered progress (the reddened lower part of the pillars may have resulted from the burning of the first roof). The nave arches were ornamented, in contrast to those at the east end, and the north aisle has some fine decorated capitals (fig. 10). The nave's unique Norman design may have been part of Serlo's original plan, even though he did not live to see it completed. It had the traditional three tiers of openings, but at Gloucester the arches opening into the aisles were greatly heightened and supported on round, 9-metre-high (30 feet) columns (see back cover); instead of a gallery there was a triforium (arched wall passage) only 3 metres (10 feet) high. At Mont St Michel, where Serlo came from, there is also a triforium rather than a gallery in the nave. The inspiration for round columns may have come from Burgundy via the bishop's chapel built in the 1080s at Hereford. The Gloucester design was also used at Tewkesbury Abbey, which was begun 1087 and completed in 1123. The Gloucester nave vault may have been of wood initially and then soon

rebuilt in stone; nothing survives because it was replaced in 1242. However, the original Romanesque rib vault of the north aisle can still be seen (fig. 11). The west end of the nave terminated with a central entrance flanked by two great towers. One of the Gloucester towers collapsed in 1164; any remaining parts of the towers were removed when the west end was rebuilt in the fifteenth century.

The church would have contained treasures in the form of hangings, fittings, lamps, reliquaries and processional crosses. One item has survived: an altar candlestick made of copper alloy with a high silver content and covered with decoration showing beasts and human figures enmeshed in foliage (fig. 12). The inscription records the commission by Abbot Peter (1107–13) and adds (in Latin): 'This flood of light, this work of virtue, bright with holy doctrine instructs us, so that Man shall not be benighted in vice.' The candlestick did not remain long at Gloucester; it was in the possession of Le Mans Cathedral from the late twelfth century and was purchased by the Victoria and Albert Museum in 1861.

Another of the cathedral's Norman treasures is the Lancaut font, although this has only been in the cathedral for about seventy years. The abbey of Gloucester, as a monastic establishment rather than a parish church, would not have had a font. The font was made in the twelfth century for the little church of St James at Lancaut (now a picturesque ruin close to the River Wye on the Mercian border with Wales). Six fonts made using the same mould survive today in various Gloucestershire churches. Sections were cast flat and then bent round and soldered together to form a tub. The Lancaut font is decorated with ten arches containing foliage decoration and seated figures in alternation; the latter probably represent apostles. When Lancaut church was destroyed, in about 1865, the font came into the possession of the Marling family of King's Stanley, who restored it in

Fig. 11
The Norman north
aisle with its rib vault,
completed in about
1120.

1890. The diocese of Gloucester in the early
twentieth century disputed the ownership; finally,
in 1940, the Marlings gave it to the cathedral.

The abbey buildings

Just as the church had a traditional Benedictine
layout, so too did the other abbey buildings. These
would typically include a cloister (often south of
the church), chapter house, refectory for communal
meals, and dormitory, together with a range of
rooms for guests and apartments for the abbot. At
Gloucester all these were provided. Serlo's monks may
have made do with the Anglo-Saxon buildings for a
time, but as soon as possible a new cloister was laid
out; this was on the north side, perhaps because there
were Anglo-Saxon buildings still in use occupying
the southern side or, more likely, to provide access to
a water supply. North of the church, passageways gave
access to the cloister. These passageways were the
inner and outer parlours (*locutoria*), where the
monks were allowed to talk with each other and with
visitors; the parlours were provided with a bench on
each side (fig. 13). They must have been rather bleak
places, not designed to encourage prolonged
sociability. The outer parlour (now usually called
the 'west slype') was next to the great courtyard, the
public area of the abbey, so it was here that monks
met visitors from the outside world.

On the east side of the cloister was the chapter
house (fig. 14), where the monks met to receive
instructions from their abbot and to transact
business. The west wall of the chapter house shows
two phases of building, the earliest reddened by
burning from a fire in the early twelfth century.
The chapter house originally had an apsidal east
end where the abbot had his seat, facing his monks,
who sat on benches below arcaded recesses along
the sides.

North of the chapter house was the dormitory
(*dorter*), which was on an upper floor, with privies

Fig. 12
The Gloucester
Candlestick (now in the
Victoria and Albert
Museum) was given to
the abbey by Abbot
Peter (1107–13).

Fig. 13
The Norman outer parlour (west slype), where the monks were allowed to meet with visitors.

(*reredorter*) on the ground floor. At Gloucester there is no sign that there was ever a 'night stair' leading directly from the dormitory to the church, as there was in some Benedictine monasteries. For their night office at 2.30 in the morning the monks would have had to descend to the cloister to enter the church. On the north side of the cloister was the refectory, where the monks assembled for meals. The dormitory and refectory were rebuilt in the thirteenth century and demolished at the Dissolution.

The south cloister walk, against the church, usually contained study cubicles, which were at first open to the weather via an arcade of arches. Not surprisingly, in later versions arrangements were made for glazing. At Gloucester the cloister has been replaced twice: once in the thirteenth century and then again in the late fourteenth. The outline cloister plan has not changed, though the Norman walks were probably narrower.

The abbey's great wealth lay in its extensive possessions of land, and careful records were kept of estates, their value, rents and management. When old records wore out, new copies were made. Very little of this enormous archive of books and papers exists today. One survivor is a volume recording grants of land and property, known as a cartulary, of 337 leaves or 'folios'. It passed at the Dissolution into lay hands, then to the dukes of Norfolk, and is now in the National Archives. It is beautifully written on vellum (calfskin) and seems to have been created around 1300. The first entry is a grant to the abbey by Henry II (1154–89); the initial letter H is decorated with a picture of a Benedictine monk receiving a charter from the king, so emphasising the abbey's dependence on royal sanction (fig. 15). The document confirms a grant already made by Henry's grandfather Henry I (1100–35) to the abbot and monks, exempting them from market tolls in Gloucester. This was a valuable concession in the town where the abbey's estate produce was traded, though the agreement was to cause ill feeling between town and abbey in later years.

Even more vital, the next item confirmed the

Fig. 14
The west end of the
Norman chapter house.
The masonry on the
left conceals the
fourteenth-century
staircase giving access
to the library.

abbey's right, established thirty years earlier, to make use of the Fulbrook stream, which was diverted through the abbey buildings. Access to its own water supply was vitally important to the abbey. The stream was not fit for drinking, having already passed through Gloucester's industrial suburb, but its main purpose was to carry off waste via a network of culverts. Water for consumption probably came from wells; there is still one in the cloister. In the thirteenth century the abbey installed a 'conduit of living water' (spring water brought in by lead pipes), which was to provide water to the abbey precinct until the seventeenth century. The water flowed into lead tanks, some of which would have been above the monks' washing place (*lavatorium*) (see fig. 38).

The abbot's lodging was next to the outer parlour, on the west side of the cloister. The twelfth-century version was a square three-storey building, today incorporated into the building called Church House. Over the outer parlour is the abbot's chapel, with a tunnel vault and Norman capitals. The abbot's

lodging has been rebuilt reusing Norman and later decoration; for instance, the gable with chevron ornament is not Norman but was re-erected on top of a thirteenth-century western extension (see fig. 39). In the fourteenth century a new and spacious lodging was built north of the infirmary, and the old building was assigned to the abbot's deputy, the prior. At the Dissolution, and with the creation of a bishopric, the newer, fourteenth-century abbot's lodging became the Bishop's Palace. This was rebuilt in the late nineteenth century and is now the King's School.

The thirteenth century

The mightily unpopular King John died in 1216 and was buried at Worcester. The country was in crisis, with Prince Louis of France in control of much of the south-east of the country and King John's son Henry only nine years old. Prompt action was needed, and the young king's supporters arranged for him to be crowned at the nearest secure centre, Gloucester

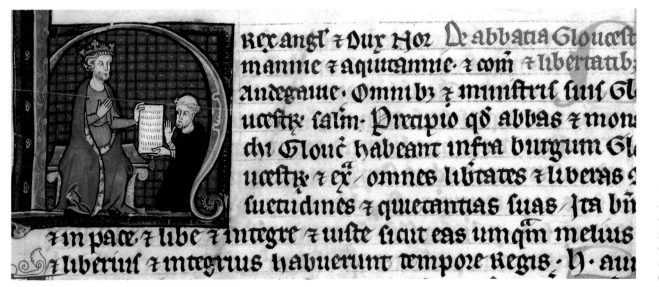

Abbey. The crown was a simple gold circlet, said to be part of his mother's headdress. The reign of Henry III was to be long (1216–72; fig. 16), and the thirteenth century was a time of growing prosperity and population. The king often visited Gloucester and rebuilt the castle. Much rebuilding also took place at the abbey. This was in the style that we now call 'Early English', using pointed arches (more flexible for the vaulting of uneven spaces), rib vaulting and complex arch-mouldings. Little of it has survived today, a notable exception being the nave vault, finished in 1242. This was constructed without the height of the Norman nave walls being raised, so the vault appears rather low. The workmanship included careful copying and matching of the Romanesque chevron ornament; for instance, zigzag ornament was copied and placed round the base of the vault shafts. These were of polished lias stone from the Forest of Dean.

Also created in the thirteenth century was the effigy of Robert, duke of Normandy (c.1050–1143; fig. 17). His nickname, Curthose ('Shortsocks'), related to his physical stature. Robert was the eldest son of William the Conqueror and, on the Conqueror's death in 1087, inherited Normandy, while his brother William Rufus gained the throne of England and reigned as William II. In 1095 Robert was a principal leader of the First Crusade, which achieved, with terrible slaughter, its aim of capturing Jerusalem from the Turks. Though apparently a brave

and decisive commander in warfare, Robert was politically outmanoeuvred by his brothers. When he returned to England in 1100, after William Rufus had been killed, his younger brother Henry I had already claimed the throne. The ensuing negotiations and struggles between the brothers ended with the defeat of Robert at the Battle of Tinchebray in 1106. He was imprisoned for the rest of his life and died in 1134 in Cardiff Castle at the advanced age of eighty-three. He was buried 'with due honour … in front of the high altar' at Gloucester Abbey. The probable site of the burial is today marked by plain tiles in the Victorian floor. It has been questioned whether it would have been possible to inter a body in the stone vaulting of the crypt, but there are precedents elsewhere and there is just sufficient space. Whatever the original grave marker, in the thirteenth century it was replaced by a wooden effigy carved from Irish bog oak, which is now in the south quire ambulatory. The overall pose and the style of armour link it to the reign of Henry III. The colouring has been redone over the centuries but represents the original splendour. The tomb chest below the effigy (perhaps 150 or 200 years later in date) displays heraldic arms and nine figures representing the ideals of chivalry.

The effigy is evidence of thirteenth-century devotion to the embellishment of Gloucester Abbey and the commemoration of its royal connections. There must once have been much more work of this date. There is a fine thirteenth-

Fig. 17
Thirteenth-century effigy of Robert Curthose, on a fifteenth-century tomb chest.

century screen (fig. 18), now situated in the north transept: its original position is obscure, though it may have been moved here from the Lady Chapel built in the 1220s, about which nothing is known. The screen was never finished and has been cut down to fit in its present position.

In the early thirteenth century the precinct of the abbey was extended to the north, and there was space for more abbey buildings. The infirmary, of which only a few arches remain, was for the care of sick monks. It consisted of an arcaded hall very like a church, with the side-aisles partitioned for more privacy. There was also an 'infirmary cloister', a small version of the great cloister where sick monks might walk in seclusion and where herbs were probably grown. West of the infirmary is a range of buildings with many medieval walls and details incorporated in them; these were originally the domestic quarters of the monastery, converted to dwellings at the Dissolution.

The south aisle of the church threatened to collapse in the early fourteenth century, probably as a result of subsidence in the foundations. The interior retains the Norman shafts and capitals, but the outer wall-face was rebuilt with pointed windows and flying buttresses, the first use in Gloucester of the architectural style sometimes known as 'Early English Decorated'. The six windows have a complex tracery design, and each is ornamented with ball-flower decoration. Though time-consuming to carve (each one takes about three hours), this basically simple motif is capable of many variations, and the effect on the abbey's south aisle must have been spectacular. Some of that effect is visible today, owing to restoration of the buttresses, which now look much as they did in 1318, the year that the south aisle was rebuilt 'with great expenditure on many items' (see fig. 111). The new work was designed to receive a sequence of statues; it is not certain that these were put in place. The three statues that survive may be of much later medieval date. Completion of the new south front was a splendid beginning to the era of Gothic architecture that was to transform the church.

CAROLYN HEIGHWAY

Fig. 18
Thirteenth-century
stone screen in the
north transept, which
now forms the entrance
to the Treasury through
a doorway made in 1973.

Fig. 19
Drawing of the
Gloucester skyline
including the abbey
(on the left) and
the castle. From a
thirteenth-century
manuscript of Geoffrey
of Monmouth's *Historia
regum Britanniae.*

EDWARD II AND THE ABBEY TRANSFORMED

IN THE SOUTH AISLE of the cathedral is a Victorian window (fig. 20) depicting what is probably the most significant event in the history of St Peter's Abbey until its dissolution. It shows Abbot Thokey receiving the body of King Edward II in October 1327. By coincidence, the window is placed almost beneath the point where the line of ball-flowers in the vault of the south aisle suddenly stutters and stops. With hindsight this takes on a symbolic significance, representing one style of building being replaced by another.

The burial of Edward II

The burial of Edward II at Gloucester is important for two reasons: first, it marks the introduction to the West Country of a wholly new style of architecture, now known as Perpendicular, which had previously been seen only in London; and second, it ensured the ultimate survival of the church itself. When Henry VIII dissolved the abbey community, he wanted the building that housed the tomb of his ancestor to be saved from destruction.

Edward II was born in 1284 and reigned from 1307 to 1327. His temperament made him unsuited to the role of a medieval king, especially as he grew up in the shadow of his macho warrior father, Edward I. Edward II was not inclined towards the kingly pursuit of warfare, and he alienated the nobility who had been his father's supporters and comrades in arms. Instead, he was strongly influenced by a succession of personal favourites, whom he showered with honours. Towards the end of his reign he became a tyrant, with no support among the ruling classes. Roger Mortimer, one of the disaffected noblemen, became the lover of Edward's queen, Isabella. Together they formed an alliance of interests, which forced Edward to abdicate early in 1327, and they then ruled the country in the name of Edward and Isabella's teenage son, who was proclaimed Edward III (1327–77).

The deposed king was brought to Berkeley Castle in the spring of 1327 and was held prisoner there. Berkeley is about 16 miles south of Gloucester and was the seat of Thomas Berkeley, Roger Mortimer's son-in-law. In the summer there was an attempt to rescue Edward. He escaped but was brought back to the castle. On 23 September Mortimer and Isabella were informed that Edward had died two days earlier. Over the last 150 years there has been much interest

Fig. 20
Abbot Thokey receives the body of King Edward II (depicted in nineteenth-century stained glass).

Fig. 21
The tomb of King
Edward II in the north
ambulatory.

in the fate of Edward II: was he murdered, as is almost certain, or did he escape from Berkeley Castle to wander through Europe, perhaps even meeting his son and dying eventually in Italy? What is beyond doubt is that on 20 December 1327 a truly magnificent funeral was held in St Peter's Abbey, Gloucester.

The coffin was placed under the floor in a position near the high altar – covered at first with just a plain slab. Some time afterwards, presumably on the orders of the young Edward III, a magnificent tomb was erected over it (fig. 21). It is believed that the tomb was designed by a London master mason. The canopy is of local Cotswold limestone, the base is faced with Purbeck marble, and the effigy is made of alabaster from the Nottingham area (the earliest use of this material for the tomb of an English monarch). Beneath what has been described as one of the most shrine-like of tomb canopies, the king is depicted as a calm and saintly figure with angels at his head; he holds a sceptre and an orb – the first orb to appear on an English royal tomb.

In the Middle Ages this tomb would have been a spectacular sight. The king's robe was painted red; his hair and beard and the lion at his feet were gilded. Precious stones set in his crown and jewelled gifts sent by members of the royal family would have sparkled in the candlelight. In 1343 young King Edward sent a model ship made of gold, which perhaps sat on the plinth that survives at the front of the tomb. Plinths and fixing points for sixteen statues can still be seen around the base. These figures, known as 'weepers', probably represented relatives of the deceased and would have been painted and gilded.

For some decades after the death of Edward II his tomb was a focus for pilgrims and travellers who brought gifts to the abbey, and the occasional miracle was reported there. (Edward's great-grandson Richard II petitioned the pope to canonise his forebear, but to no avail.) In 2008 this internationally important monument was the subject of an intensive conservation project. The structure was stabilised, earlier repairs were reworked, and the whole monument was cleaned.

The burial of Edward II brought Gloucester Abbey into the world of the royal court. His son Edward III, only fourteen at the time of his father's death, had within three years taken control of the kingdom. He instigated the arrest and execution of Roger Mortimer in 1330, and the banishment from court of Queen Isabella. Attention was then focused on the abbey – now the resting place of a king – and on the question of an appropriate setting for a royal tomb.

Transforming the east end

The transformation of the east end of Gloucester Abbey into a suitable setting for the tomb of Edward II began with the south transept, probably in the spring of 1331. The young Edward III was now in control of the kingdom and was concerned to establish the importance of his dynasty, the Plantagenets. The magnificent tomb of his father and the enhancement of its setting over the next twenty-five years may be seen as part of this policy. Chroniclers emphasised that it was the gifts brought by pilgrims to the royal tomb that paid for the work. However, taking into account the involvement of the royal court, the personal interest of Edward III and the employment of royal designers, more recent commentators have also emphasised the role of royal patronage.

The abbey in 1331 was still essentially the Norman structure of the early twelfth century, with the east end probably unchanged since the time of Serlo. The presbytery and quire would have appeared very dark and old-fashioned, especially in comparison with great churches such as Worcester Cathedral, where the old Norman east end had been totally demolished and rebuilt in the thirteenth century. Similar works were not carried out at Gloucester, as royal architects from London had developed a building style that could be used to transform the

existing structure, avoiding the need to replace it. This was the style now known as Perpendicular, and it could be achieved by applying panels of fine stone tracery to existing Norman-built walls (fig. 22).

English Perpendicular is a style of architecture characterised by what looks like a cage of tracery. Thin shafts of masonry run vertically from floor to vault – over the openings of galleries and through high-level windows – and strong horizontal lines create an overall grid pattern. It derives from the French style known as Rayonnant, which originated in the Paris area in the mid-thirteenth century. In London, nearly a hundred years later, architects employed by the royal court were developing it further. They were working on St Stephen's Chapel in the Palace of Westminster and on the chapter house

Fig. 22
Early Perpendicular panelling in the south transept.

Fig. 23
The experimental lierne vault of the south transept.

of St Paul's Cathedral. Only the much-altered crypt of St Stephen's survives today, and Old St Paul's was destroyed in the Great Fire of London. The work in the south transept at Gloucester is therefore the oldest surviving example of a style that would dominate English architecture until the Reformation. Perpendicular found its most elaborate expression in a trio of royal buildings: King's College Chapel, Cambridge (1448–1515), St George's Chapel, Windsor (1475–1528), and the Henry VII Chapel in Westminster Abbey (1503–08).

The Perpendicular architecture of Gloucester's south transept must be regarded as experimental. The use of applied panelling and the earliest appearance of a new feature in building – the four-centred arch – make the south transept of particular interest to architectural historians. No document names the architect, but the fact that some of the details here are also found in Kent strengthens the claim of Thomas of Canterbury to have been its initial designer (and probably also the architect of

the tomb of Edward II). Thomas died in 1336, and it has been suggested that the south transept vault (fig. 23) was designed by a local man, John de Sponlee. This is an elaborate lierne vault (liernes being thin, almost matchstick-like, ribs that perform no structural function). The architect of the vault chose to dispense with the roof bosses normally used to cover the joins where ribs meet; we can assume this experiment did not prove popular, as it was not copied elsewhere.

On the east wall of the south transept is a memorial known as the 'Apprentice Bracket' (fig. 26). It appears to show a young man – beardless, with long, flowing hair – falling from the vault above. Watching is a grief-stricken older man, identified as the master mason by his bag of tools. We do not know whether it is a memorial to an individual or to all those workmen killed or injured during the building work.

Following the work in the south transept, the remodelling programme moved to the quire and the presbytery. Two abbots were responsible here: Adam

Fig. 24
Christ in majesty is surrounded by an angel orchestra.

Fig. 25
Gloucester's 'flying spans' were designed during the remodelling of the quire.

Sketch of old Norman Choir showing how it was cased by Abbot Staunton. 1337–1351.

Fig. 26
A master mason and an apprentice are depicted on this fourteenth-century stone bracket.

Fig. 27
F. S. Waller's drawing of 1890 shows how the Perpendicular panelling was applied to the Norman quire.

de Staunton (1337–51) and Thomas Horton (1351–77). The architecture was neither an experiment in Perpendicular nor the full flowering of the style but rather the confident execution of something mature and understood. The vault is not a fan vault – that would come later – and is in a West Country style (fig. 24). With three long ribs along the ridge, the ribbing has the appearance of a net pinned with bosses to the vault, and its impact is breathtaking. Very slender 'flying spans' cross the high arches on the north and south sides of the crossing (fig. 25). These are not structural – they are too fine to carry the weight of the vault and indeed seem barely thick enough to carry their own weight – but they allow the visual pattern of the vault to be continuous and for it to be the same height from one end of the quire to the other. Sculptors created over 400 bosses for the astonishingly complex quire vault, and over the high altar is the figure of Christ in majesty, who is surrounded by carved figures of angels, many of them playing musical instruments.

What is amazing is the audacious treatment of the old Norman building (fig. 27). In the ambulatory the fronts of piers were sliced off to provide a flat surface, the whole of the roof was removed, and the east end of the building was demolished (fig. 28). The question is: how did the builders know that the structure would remain standing? The truth is that they did not, as Gloucester's present-day master mason Paschal Mychalysin explains: 'They had to go through a system of trial and error because there was no knowledge of structural engineering on which they could base their calculation.'

The working practices of medieval craftsmen are sometimes described as if each man was allowed to follow his own design preference. This was clearly very far from the case here. Masons, carpenters and painters on glass worked in harmony, using the same design motifs. The pinnacled wooden canopies of the monks' stalls are repeated in the Great East Window – painted in glass – and they echo those in stone on the tomb canopy of the king. The quatrefoil frieze carved in wood across the stalls continues in stone around the east end.

The beautiful canopies over the monks' stalls were made locally, it has been suggested, to designs by royal carpenters. More informal are the misericords (or 'mercy seats'). Medieval monks were required to spend many hours of each day at services in the quire, and for this they were required to stand. When tipped, each hinged seat provided a ledge for perching on. The under-sides of these seats could be

Fig. 28
Behind the new Perpendicular panelling, the Norman north ambulatory is hardly altered.

Fig. 29
An elephant carved on a medieval misericord.

carved (fig. 29), and here the craftsmen do seem to have been free to choose their subjects. Gloucester's fifty-eight misericords do not include any of the scurrilous or bawdy scenes often found in other churches. On the contrary, they contain a higher proportion of religious subjects than is usual. The carving is exuberant, and there is a wide range of subjects: biblical scenes, folk tales, history, legend and sport.

The tile-maker's craft is represented in the quire by the fifteenth-century pavement on the sanctuary steps. This was made during the abbacy of Thomas Seabroke (1450–57). In the nineteenth century medieval tiles were removed from various places in the cathedral and relaid in the tribune gallery.

Precious metals and textiles once played a part in the religious ceremonial. Gold and silver vessels,

processional crosses studded with jewels, and elaborate and expensive ecclesiastical robes can be seen painted in the medieval windows, but they were lost to us at the dissolution of the monastery. There is just a reminder of them in the two large fourteenth-century wooden cope chests in the south ambulatory (see fig. 6), which once contained the gorgeous embroidered ceremonial robes of the medieval abbots.

The final building phase in the east end of the monastic church was the remodelling of the north transept in the new Perpendicular style. We know that this was done between 1368 and 1374, at a cost of £718 1s. 2d., of which Abbot Horton himself paid

£444 0s. 2d. Thus the east end of Gloucester Abbey was transformed, to provide a fit setting for the body of Edward II.

Gloucester has a further royal connection. In 1378 the boy king Richard II held a parliament in Gloucester, in the great hall built by Abbot Horton. On its site is now a fifteenth-century building (on an older undercroft), which is still called the Parliament Room. It is believed that Richard's own badge – the white hart – was painted on pillars either side of the tomb of Edward II, to mark this royal visit. The abbey's chronicler tells us that the monastery was so crowded that it was 'more like a market than a house

Fig. 30
Tiers of figures rise from earth to heaven in the Great East Window of the quire.

Fig. 31
Christ and the Virgin are
side by side; she is
crowned and his hand is
raised in blessing.

Fig. 32
The famous
Gloucester 'golfer'.

of religion. For the green of the cloister was so flat-
tened by wrestlings and ball games that it was hope-
less to expect any grass to be left there.'

The Great East Window

The great window that forms the east wall of the
presbytery is an artistic and technological achievement which astonishes the modern visitor. It is almost impossible to imagine the impact it must have
had on monks and pilgrims in the fourteenth century. The decision to replace the east end with a wall
of glass was daring. On completion it was the largest
window anyone had ever seen; at 72 feet (22 metres)
high and 38 feet (12 metres) wide, it is the size of a
tennis court. The overall frame stands broader than
the walls of the presbytery, so that the outer edges
are not visible from a distance and the window appears to float unsupported. It has a restrained colour

scheme, with a high proportion of shimmering silvery glass. Bands of expensive red and blue glass run vertically upwards, and tier upon tier of sculpture-like figures rise up from behind the high altar to the angel-filled heavens in the vault above (fig. 30).

No record has survived of the commission, or the date of the window or where it was made. The most likely workshop for a commission on this scale would have been Bristol, and similarities in style have been identified with work in what is now Bristol Cathedral, and in Tewkesbury Abbey. The characteristics of this style include faces with eyes cast down and glancing sideways – an expression that we might describe as 'glum' – elongated fingers and toes, and an S-shaped body. One of the figures portrayed is St George, who is wearing a style of armour that can be dated to the 1350s; this ties in with the dates of Abbot Horton, who is said to have been responsible for completing the presbytery.

The figures are depicted standing in niches; above each is a canopy, which rises to become the pedestal of the figure above. These painted architectural features emulate a real stone structure, showing as they do the under-sides of the canopies in an early attempt at perspective. The figures themselves have the appearance of beautiful stone sculptures, delicately coloured with yellow stain, and with touches of green, murrey (mauve) and pot-metal yellow. The subject of the window appears to be the coronation of the Virgin. She is depicted on Christ's right hand; he is turned towards her, raising his hand in blessing (fig. 31). The theme of the window is hierarchy; heaven and earth are shown to be linked through a structure of ascending stages of holiness.

At the lowest level are the shields and coats of arms of noble families who were supporters of Edward III in his French wars, and who may well have contributed to the cost of the window itself. These include the earls of Arundel, Warwick and Pembroke, as well as the Black Prince. Among them

Fig. 33
Silver stain is skilfully used in the figure of St Lawrence (*far left*).

Fig. 34
St Thomas is one of the best-preserved figures in the Great East Window.

Fig. 35
St John has a fierce eagle and remarkably large feet!

is a curious anomaly: a roundel containing a figure of a man in peasant costume hitting a ball with a curved stick. This is the Gloucester 'golfer' (fig. 32). In fact, we cannot be certain of what the figure is doing or why he is included in the window. It would be nice to believe he is the one representative of the common man in the window's hierarchical structure, but whether he is playing a forgotten medieval game or demonstrating how to keep wolves away from sheep we shall probably never know.

The next level of the window contains figures that are usually accepted as being abbots of Gloucester and bishops of Worcester and Hereford, in alternating positions. The artist has used repeat drawings for his figures here, varying the details to give them some individuality, and in some cases reversing them. There are three figures of kings in the centre of this row. Two of them look out of scale and were probably recycled from the original clerestory scheme, where kings and other benefactors were almost certainly shown, but one – that of Edward II – may have had an original place of honour here. Above the abbots and bishops stand the saints, female and male in alternate positions. Each is identified by an 'attribute': for example, St Margaret of Antioch spears her dragon and St Lawrence holds a small gridiron to represent the one on which he was martyred (fig. 33).

The central figures of the fourth tier are those of Christ and the Virgin. Originally both were sitting on thrones, but the lower panel of the Christ figure has been replaced. On either side of them are apostles with their attributes: St Peter has a church and a key, St Thomas a spear (fig. 34), St Paul a sword, and St John the Evangelist a palm and an eagle (fig. 35). There are angels in the tier above (with an intruded picture of the Virgin and Child). At the very top we see not God, as we might expect, but a portrait of St Clement – a piece of fifteenth-century glass perhaps put in after the dissolution as a replacement for a broken light.

The best-preserved figures in this great window – St Thomas, St James the Less and St Cecilia among them – are outstanding works of art. The yellow-stained hair, the composition of the drapery, the fine details in the borders and the graceful S-shape of the figures stand comparison with the finest paintings of the medieval world. However, it should not be forgotten that to the monks who prayed in this quire every day the figures portrayed were familiar, real and intimately known. Before and above them stood the predecessors of their abbot, important figures in their history, beloved saints and revered apostles, linking their world to the heavenly kingdom.

The Gloucester quire is a soaring space, yet an intimate and enclosed one. It has the feeling of a church-within-a-church, and indeed that is what it was. Here, in an earthly vision of the heavenly kingdom, the monks came, eight times every twenty-four hours, to pray to God and to praise Him. And here worship has continued every day, down through the centuries.

The cloister

It is now widely accepted that the Gloucester cloister was begun during the abbacy of Thomas Horton before he remodelled the north transept and thereby completed the transformation of the east end of the church. This makes the vault of the Gloucester cloister the first full-scale structural fan vault to be found anywhere (fig. 36). Small-scale decorative fans had been used in tomb canopies before, and there used to be a view, based on an eighteenth-century engraving, that the circular chapter house at Hereford had a fan vault that pre-dated Gloucester's. This drawing is now known to be an imaginative and misguided reconstruction. In the words of Alan Brooks, 'conceived in the 1350s fan vaulting was probably invented at Gloucester'.

The origins of the fan vault are not at all clear. We may simply have to accept that the English masons were enamoured of the idea of elaborate vaults and that in the quire they had already used the maximum number of ribs that could come from one springing point. The walls and the vault of the quire

Fig. 38
The *lavatorium*, where
the monks washed
their hands, is in the
north walk.

are two different patterns, but in the cloister the designer spread the stone tracery over every wall, window and vault surface as a harmonious whole. There was also a major change of technique. In the vaults of the quire the spaces between stone ribs were filled with lighter, less finished masonry, which was subsequently plastered. The cloister vault, by contrast, is entirely formed of individual, fine-quality stone blocks, with the ribs carved on to the surface of each. This method of construction made huge technical demands of the masons and was clearly very expensive, which may explain why most of the builders of later fan vaults reverted to the use of ribs and infill. Gloucester's cloisters were built in two phases. After completion of the east walk there was a pause in the work; the other three walks were constructed in the time of Abbot Walter Froucester (1381–1412). There are subtle changes of detail marking this interruption, but nothing that detracts

from the overall harmony, proportion and beauty of this remarkable place.

For the monks the cloister was a place in which to live and work. Along the south walk are twenty-two carrels, or study booths, each with its own window (fig. 37). It is not difficult to imagine each carrel with a small desk and a monk bent over a document. One must hope it is true that there were screens at each end of this walk to defend against draughts, and that portable braziers warmed fingers that would otherwise have been too cold to write! The *lavatorium* ('washing place') in the north walk of the cloister is decorated with a delightful small-scale fan vault (fig. 38). The trough with its drainage holes would have been lead-lined, and on the shelf behind there would have been lead tanks with taps at the front. The *lavatorium* was used for hand-washing before meals. The whole community of monks would line up in order of precedence to wash and dry their

hands. They would then process in silence into the refectory. The open alcove opposite the *lavatorium* is where their towels were hung. Scratched on the stone bench that runs along the north walk of the cloister are the traces of two board games (Nine Men's Morris and Fox and Geese), which suggests that this area was used for recreation by novices and boy singers.

The west end and the tower

The next builder abbot after Walter Froucester was John Morwent (1421–37). During his abbacy the west end of the church was reconstructed, with windows in the Perpendicular style (fig. 39). The effect was to flood the west end with light. The round Norman piers were replaced with composite ones – slender shafts grouped around a central core. Above, the abbot replaced the thirteenth-century Early English vault with a much more elaborate one

decorated with striking and vigorous roof bosses. These are carved with foliage, green men (fig. 41) and mythical beasts. The central boss portrays the coronation of the Virgin, echoing the theme of the Great East Window of eighty years earlier. The new vault makes a rather abrupt transition to the older one, and it is probable that, if Abbot Morwent had lived longer, he would have remodelled the entire nave from end to end. Admirers of the Norman style are grateful that he did not get the opportunity!

Abbot Morwent's other great legacy is the south porch (fig. 40). It replaced the west door as the main entrance to the church and continues to function as such. It seems likely that the great wooden doors were moved to the porch from the west end, as the ironwork on them is from the twelfth century. The porch was heavily restored in the nineteenth century, and only a minority of its stones are actually medieval, but it is thought to be faithful to the original design.

Fig. 39
The west end, rebuilt by Abbot Morwent in the fifteenth century.

Fig. 40
The magnificent
medieval south porch,
with its nineteenth-
century sculptures.

Fig. 41
One of about forty
green men to be found
in the cathedral.

Gloucester Cathedral tower, constructed in the middle of the fifteenth century, is a landmark, which is both highly visible and astonishingly beautiful (fig. 42). The three tiers of masonry, with louvred openings and surface decoration, rise in perfect proportion to the four airy pinnacles, which seem so light and delicate they could be made of lace. The tower is 225 feet (69 metres) high. The whole structure weighs about 6,000 tons (6,096 metric tonnes) and was built on Norman foundations, which were already 350 years old when it was started. The builder was a monk of St Peter's Abbey called Robert Tully, who worked under the direction of the abbot, Thomas Seabroke (1450–57). Later in life Tully became bishop of St David's. Abbot Seabroke did not live to see his tower completed. He is buried in a chantry chapel, and his tomb has an alabaster effigy dressed in ecclesiastical robes.

Inside the tower is another great medieval treasure: the bell known as Great Peter. This is usually described as the only medieval bourdon bell in the country that can still be heard; a bourdon bell has a very deep sound. Weighing 59 cwt (about 3 metric tonnes), Great Peter still marks the hours of the day and summons people to worship as it has for nearly six centuries.

The Lady Chapel

Chapels dedicated to the Virgin Mary had been built in England since the late twelfth century, and one was built at St Peter's Abbey in the thirteenth century. During the fourteenth century magnificent Lady Chapels were built at Wells, Lichfield and Ely, and in the next century the monks at Gloucester built their own new Lady Chapel at the east end of the church (fig. 43). They were not to know it would be the very last new building of the abbey.

The Lady Chapel was begun by Abbot Hanley (1457–72) and was completed by his successor, Abbot Farley (1472–98). The symbol of Edward IV (the Yorkist white rose) can be seen in the windows of the chapel, which suggests the building was finished before the triumph of the Tudors at the Battle of Bosworth in 1485, which brought to an end the Wars of the Roses. A building date of between 1465 and 1482 is therefore generally accepted.

The design of the Lady Chapel follows closely that of the quire. However, since the panelling of the walls was not overlaid onto old Norman work, it could incorporate huge windows. The designer did not use a fan vault, which might have been expected by this date, but chose instead to match the pattern of the quire vault with its three long ridge ribs.

Today, we are impressed by the architecture, but we see it as bare stone. In the Middle Ages the architecture would have been merely the background to spectacular decoration: painted stonework framing huge windows of coloured glass, painted statues in niches and richly embroidered altar hangings. Behind the altar a screen, which now stands damaged and empty, would have contained forty statues of saints and martyrs. Their names can still be detected scratched on the niches they once occupied. As one author has remarked, 'the saints and prophets on the church walls were the Church Triumphant made actual'.

The east window of the chapel is hard to read. At first glance it looks like a kaleidoscope of coloured

glass rather than a coherent design. This is because it is made up of hundreds of pieces of medieval glass gathered from all over the building and placed here in around 1800. There are clues to the original appearance of this window (see fig. 76). The fragments that remain in their original position suggest there was an emphasis on female virgin saints; for example, St Etheldreda and St Withburga have been mooted. Figures in niches alternated with outdoor scenes, which may have depicted events in the lives of the saints. There would certainly have been an important and central representation of the Virgin Mary. The glass incorporated into the window from other sites also contains clues as to what filled the windows of the rest of the church in the Middle Ages. A set of saints under canopies, made in the fifteenth century, almost certainly came from the nave; parts of a Tree of Jesse possibly came from the north transept, and a Passion series may have been in one of the side-chapels.

Devotion to the Virgin Mary in England was demonstrated not only by the building of Lady Chapels but also through the development of a particular type of musical anthem. Whereas the monks of the medieval abbeys sang Gregorian plainsong, the songs in praise of the Virgin – 'Marian antiphons', as they are known – required a full range of voices: treble, alto, tenor and bass. This led to boys being brought in to sing in the Lady Chapel. By the middle of the fifteenth century adult male singers who were not monks would also be employed. At Gloucester two singing galleries were constructed, one on the north and one on the south, from which two choirs could sing, calling and responding to each other – 'antiphonally' – across the chapel.

Dazzling to the eye, heavy with incense and filled with glorious music for the Virgin, the Lady Chapel was intended to overwhelm the worshipper with devotional intensity.

SUSAN HAMILTON

II THE CATHEDRAL FOUNDATION

THE SURRENDER OF THE ABBEY of St Peter to Henry VIII's commissioners was a moment of shattering change. It brought to an end a long, unbroken thread of prayer and praise. It drove out the familiar sights and sounds of the life of a great abbey situated in the heart of a city. There were to be no more glimpses of tonsured monks in their habits, no constant stream of traffic through the gates. Reformation ended that, as it ended the great stream of pilgrims seeking grace. The treasures of the monastery – chalices and jewels that had glittered in the candlelight – disappeared into eager, secular hands. The treasures of the library were lost; books that had been prayed over were torn up for scrap. The change went deeper, though; long-standing relationships with the abbey's tenants, scattered over distant villages and fields, were dislocated. The merchants and tradesmen who sold goods to the abbey at the door of the slype lost business. The destitute who depended on abbey charity and the sick who got relief at the infirmary were suddenly bereft. This was a seismic shift in the life of the city and of the farms and estates around it. However, while other abbeys were closed and plundered for masonry, becoming ruins such as those at Tintern or Hailes, for St Peter's there was to be a very different future. Henry VIII elected to carve a new diocese out of the sprawling parishes of the diocese of Worcester.

A dean and a small community of canons, known as 'the chapter', moved into accommodation in the former monastic precinct, now a 'college' (fig. 44). They took over responsibility for the building and for its worship. A first bishop of Gloucester was appointed. His responsibilities lay largely in the parishes of the diocese. As bishop, though, he had a seat (his *cathedra*) within the quire and the authority to review the life of the cathedral and to see that the statutes were being observed. The cathedral is still the fixed point at the heart of the bishop's ministry; he teaches there, uniting the church in one faith. To this day bishop, dean and chapter share in the life of the cathedral and take their places in the stalls assigned to them in the quire. Where once St Peter's had been an abbey, a place set apart, a building where monks could live a cloistered life, now there was a cathedral with a new dedication, recorded in the statutes of 1544 as 'The Holy and Individed Trinity'. In time, 'Individed' was tidied up into 'Indivisible', and later, when Reformation battles were no longer being fought, the original dedication to St Peter was remembered and added in. The continuity is important. The present-day chapter is keenly aware of its Benedictine past and today sustains daily prayer and the praise of God in the spirit of those who worshipped here a thousand years ago. Benedictine ideas of hospitality are important, too, and so is the distinctive responsibility to be a cathedral that acts as a focus for the city and the diocese as well as being the seat of its bishop. Gloucester Cathedral is a place where different communities come together and acknowledge that they belong together under the sovereignty of God, which extends over all ages and all places. The modern chapter is strengthened by lay members with areas of particular expertise and supported by an energetic community of paid staff and volunteers. They are all deeply conscious of sharing in a rich inheritance and a great responsibility. Together they care for the building, welcome visitors, teach the faith and, above all, offer praise to God as they join in his mission in the world. The Reformation was a massive dislocation, but the continuities matter more.

DAVID HOYLE

Fig. 44
The west end, showing the former abbots' lodgings on the left.

REFORMATION AND CIVIL WAR

STAND INSIDE THE SOARING confidence of the Lady Chapel, where all the lines sweep up to heaven, and you will have a glimpse of what the Abbey of St Peter at Gloucester looked like just before the Reformation (fig. 45). It will only be a glimpse; long ago restorers and reformers demolished the blaze of glory that Catholics built here at the end of the fifteenth century. Then the chapel was alive with statues of the saints, stained glass and gold leaf. The presiding idea in the Catholic faith, on the eve of the Reformation, was that there is a constant traffic between heaven and earth. Prayers and pilgrimages, masses and monastic offices, the intercession of the saints and all the rituals of the Church's year with relics, candles and crosses, expressed the deep conviction that in St Peter's Abbey you stood on the very border of

Fig. 45
The east end of the Lady Chapel; seventeenth-century altar rails and a stone screen damaged by reformers can be seen.

heaven, amid great tides of grace. The building and its decoration spelt out that conviction, summoning the faithful to all the means of devotion. In the Lady Chapel there is plenty of evidence of what we had and what we have lost.

End of an era

When we write the history of the Reformation, we are forever looking for causes and for origins. We find the first reformers and root out all the critics of medieval religion; we list the ways in which the Church failed to live up to its calling, we sketch the way ideas spread within the universities and along the trade routes. Then, in Gloucester and elsewhere, we can catalogue the first cracks to appear in medieval Catholicism and the apparently irresistible rise of a different faith. We know, for example, that in Gloucester there were complaints about 'enormities' and 'disorders' in the abbey. We know that a Gloucester priest thought that we might pray until our tongues 'be worne to stumpes', but it would still not help the dead escape from purgatory. We know too that Gloucestershire produced one of the giants of the early Reformation: William Tyndale, the translator of genius who turned the Latin majesty of the Vulgate into spirited English, was born near Dursley. There is a danger, however, that when writing about the origins of Reformation we write Catholicism off and persuade ourselves that it was unpopular, corrupt and moribund. We can forget that nearly all the evidence suggests that Catholicism in 1530 was still lively, energetic and popular. Money was still being spent on St Peter's Abbey at the beginning of the sixteenth century. A little wooden chapel was built onto the back of the quire stalls in the south transept and covered with the initials of John the Baptist only a few years before Martin Luther pinned up his 'Ninety-Five Theses'. It survives to this day, a little testament to a

Fig. 46
The altar in the Chapel of St John the Baptist, south transept. The woodwork on the left was painted in the sixteenth century.

Fig. 47
Initials J. B., painted in the Chapel of St John the Baptist.

Fig. 48
The arms of Abbot
Parker from the abbey
register.

Fig. 49
The alabaster effigy of
Abbot Parker, north
quire aisle.

Catholicism that was far from defeated on the eve of Reformation (figs 46 and 47).

As Reformation began in England, there was still energy and confidence in the abbey. Whatever that Gloucester priest thought about praying for the dead, the abbot of Gloucester, William Parker (elected in 1514), was confident of the old Catholic certainties (fig. 48). He built a splendid chantry chapel complete with an alabaster effigy of himself, robed in mitre and chasuble (fig. 49). This was a place where there would be an altar and where, he anticipated, the monks of Gloucester would say Mass and pray for his soul after his death. Parker (also known as William Malverne, after his place of birth) was a prince of the Church and felt no shame in that, spending money on his lodgings near the cathedral and on a splendid home at Prinknash. He had not felt the cold wind blowing out of Luther's Germany.

'True religion, and the true worship of God'

Abbot Parker can be forgiven his misplaced confidence. No one anticipated that Henry VIII (1509–47) would turn Protestant (fig. 50). It was well known that the king's faith was rooted in tradition. In his early years he was so devoted to the papacy that he wrote a book condemning Luther and won from the pope the title Defender of the Faith. It was only as the succession crisis gathered pace and the king longed for a new queen that he saw the need to do things differently. Refused the divorce he asked for, Henry suddenly set out to sever the links that bound him to Rome. The early battles of the English Reformation were over authority not doctrine. In Gloucester the first real indication of change was not a new article of faith but the requirement that Abbot Parker and thirty-four monks take the Oath of Supremacy in the chapter house in 1534. Very soon, though, it became clear that what was intended was

Fig. 50
Portrait of Henry VIII
(oil on panel) by Holbein
the Younger, from the
collection of Castle
Howard.

far more than a bit of political and constitutional reform. The royal supremacy bit deep into old certainties about the unity of Christendom. Suddenly the papacy was perceived to be just another foreign power, and service books had to be defaced so that all references to the pope could be swept away, prayers were changed and the Church was nationalised. Still, presumably, Parker hoped to cling to the old ways typified by his chantry chapel. When the king visited Gloucester in 1535, Parker was there to meet him, vested in the traditional way. A year later the Ten Articles reasserted some familiar beliefs and encouraged the conservatives to believe that reform was reaching its limits and that the statues of the saints and the prayers for the dead might stay.

Other signs, however, were much less encouraging. The religious calendar was changed, and familiar holy days were abolished. By 1536 English bibles were appearing in churches (fig. 51), and, much more disturbing, in the same year some small monastic houses were suppressed. Monasteries had been dissolved before. There was a widespread recognition that some of them needed reform and a few were beyond help. Critics were more eager to spend money on education and on charity than on plump priors. There was general assent that it was time to rationalise and reform. However, Thomas Cromwell, the king's principal secretary, was proposing something altogether more aggressive and alarming. In 1536 and 1537 he moved decisively against a number of communities, including the Augustinian house of St Oswald's, whose ruins can still be seen a few hundred yards to the north-west of the cathedral (fig. 52). Even at this stage no one really foresaw the scale of destruction to come. Monasticism still had plenty of supporters, and there were a number of houses where discipline and piety were strong. Suddenly, however, all that confidence leached away. Monks despaired in the face of scathing criticism from evangelical preachers.

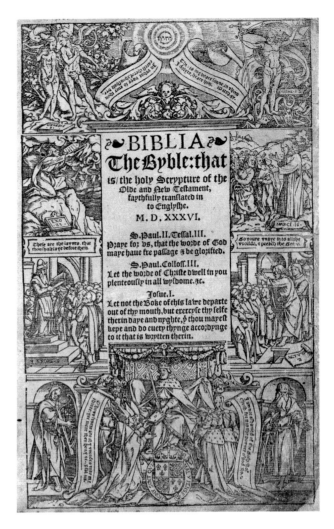

Fig. 51
Frontispiece of the Gloucester Cathedral Coverdale Bible, in English, 1536.

Donors, eager to secure a toehold in eternity, began to wonder if there was any future in an abbey, and now even the great houses looked vulnerable. In 1539 the second Act of Dissolution confirmed the king's title to monastic property, and the commissioners appointed to supervise the dissolution became more active. The greater monastic houses fell one by one. Locally, Cirencester, Llanthony Secunda, Hailes and Winchcombe were dissolved in 1539. Then, in January 1540, the commissioners turned their attention to Gloucester.

Abbot Parker was not there to meet them. There is an old story that he had fled, a contumacious Catholic to the end. The truth is rather more prosaic: he had died in the early summer of 1539 and, in the chaos of the times, seems never to have been placed in the splendour of the tomb that he had so carefully planned. It was left to the prior to hand over the keys

Fig. 52
Ruins of St Oswald's
Augustinian Priory,
founded c.900. It was
briefly a parish church
after the Dissolution.

Fig. 53
The initial letter 'T' in
the grant of arms to the
dean and chapter of
Gloucester, 1542.

to the abbey, on 3 January 1540. Thirty monks were there to be granted pensions, in addition to a truly startling eighty-six servants and twenty-three officers of the household. The possessions of the monastery were valued at £1,952 10s. 11¾d. One or two local houses were richer – Hailes and Glastonbury, for example – but to get the real measure of the wealth and importance of the abbey it helps to know that in the same year Deerhurst, an abbey a few miles to the north, was valued at £134. In 1535 St Oswald's annual income was assessed at just £90.

For the Catholic community the losses were bitter to bear, but at least the building was saved. King Henry created a new diocese, and the abbey church was made into a cathedral, teaching a new faith (fig. 53). The rhetoric surrounding the new foundation was full of enthusiasm for piety and true doctrine as is revealed in the Royal Charter:

We, being influenced by divine goodness, and desiring above all things, that true religion, and the true worship of God may not only not be abolished, but entirely restored to the primitive and genuine rule of simplicity [have] endeavoured to the utmost that for the future the pure word of God may be taught in that place.

The building's survival had more to do with pedigree than piety. Henry VIII, with all his passion for dynasty, knew very well that one of his 'renowned ancestors', Edward II, was buried in Gloucester and that the abbey was really a kind of chapel royal. He had no intention of pulling the roof down on his own house. As a result, in 1541 Gloucester acquired a dean and a chapter in place of an abbot, a prior and the monks. The first dean, William Jennings, was no stranger to the place; he had been prior of the nearby house of St Oswald's. It is unlikely that his conscience troubled him very much as he made a quick accommodation with the new religion and the new realities. He was to prove remarkably flexible in his opinions not just once but again and again, as he negotiated the lurching reformations of Edward VI, Queen Mary and Queen Elizabeth and held on to his deanery into infirm old age. The first bishop, John Wakeman, was another survivor of the old religion; he had been the last abbot of Tewkesbury. These continuities must not be allowed to blind us to the all the changes that were taking place. Buildings were pulled down, rents had been lost, the community was a shadow of its former size and there was also a new school to house. In Gloucester, as elsewhere, Henry VIII diverted some of the wealth prised from the grip of the monks into the fashionable new enthusiasm for teaching boys to read and write. The College School, later known as the King's School, was part of the new foundation; its head teacher, the 'archididasculus', had his payments recorded in the chapter account books.

Fig. 54
Illustration from Foxe's *Book of Martyrs*. At the top sacred objects are being carried to a bonfire.

Old and new rubbed along uneasily, and Gloucester watched and waited as it got the measure of the new foundation and the new beliefs.

The stripping of the altars

It was a curious beginning in the new cathedral. The service books of the old faith had been burnt, but there was nothing to take their place. It took four years for the king to provide the dean and chapter with a set of statutes to guide them. The initial hesitations were misleading, though; reform was on its way, and it was carrying a hammer (fig. 54). Chantries were abolished, so there were no further Masses said in Abbot Seabroke's little chapel. There was not even an altar placed in poor Abbot Parker's chantry. Thanks largely to Archbishop Cranmer's efforts, English services were eventually published and had to be used; statues were taken down, candles and candlesticks, crosses and vestments were removed; even the wall paintings were scraped away, as a new orthodoxy beat out the beauty of holiness. At some point a terrible destructive force swept through the Lady Chapel, shattering not just the statues on the screen behind the altar but even the niches in which they stood. Images fell from the windows too, in a carnival of righteous indignation (fig. 55). It is likely that the work was done during the reign of Edward VI (1547–53), when reformers were first let out of cautious confinement. Iconoclasts are not good record-keepers, however, and we do not know who did the damage or when; it is possible that the Lady Chapel screen survived the early Reformation but was destroyed by Puritan zeal during the Civil War.

Bishop Hooper

Somewhere near the forefront of all this Protestant reform was one of Gloucester's most famous bishops, John Hooper (1552–55). Born, we think, in Somerset,

Fig. 55
Carving of an angel with missing head over the door to the crypt.

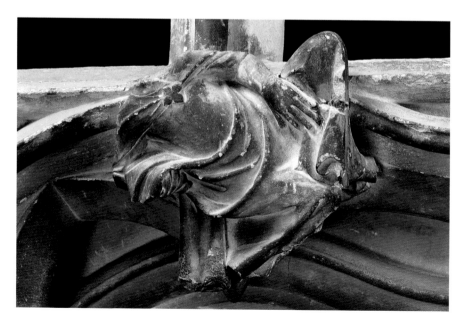

an only son with a lofty sense of vocation and destiny, Hooper was educated at Oxford and then became a Cistercian monk at Cleeve in Somerset. Just as a glittering career began to open up before this ambitious man, something forced him to think again and turn back to his books. He read the Swiss reformers Zwingli and Bullinger and looked again at scripture. He was persuaded to Protestantism by all that reading. It was a scholar's conversion.

However he got there, he arrived with conviction. He was soon much too radical for Oxford. He crossed swords with Stephen Gardiner, the bishop of Winchester, and had to escape. He went abroad, to the great cities of Reformation, first to Strasbourg, where he took a Protestant wife, and then to Zurich, where he forged a friendship with one of the giants of the Reformation, Heinrich Bullinger. When the time came to leave Zurich, it was to Bullinger that he confided a startling prophecy: 'You shall hear of me to be burnt to ashes and that shall be the last news.' Hooper returned to London, and now, during a more radical phase of the English Reformation, his star rose. He gave crowded lectures and preached at court. Then in 1551 he was made bishop of Gloucester.

He was an extraordinarily angular character. He objected to the reformed vestments of the Church of England and would not wear them; he even objected to the service used to make him bishop. Once in Gloucester, he harried the clergy into better preaching and set them tests to see how well they knew the Bible. In Hooper we see the new, single-minded focus on holy writ that was characteristic of so much Protestant thought. He was dismayed to discover a large number of his clergy could not remember the Ten Commandments. He was passionate for scripture and for pure doctrine. He was serious, determined and never learned to bite his tongue. Convinced that too much of the old superstition survived in the prayers and pilgrimages of the past, he castigated what he called 'a mixed and mingled religion'.

His days as bishop were short and sharp. At the accession of the Catholic Queen Mary (1553–58; fig. 57) he was quickly identified as an enemy of Church and state and was imprisoned. Years of reform were overturned in an instant. The Mass was back, and so were the saints. The blessed sacrament was now restored to the high altar and a candle burnt before it. A new bishop was appointed in Hooper's place – James Brookes, a man who took a seat at the trial of Archbishop Cranmer. The new Catholic establishment hoped to persuade Hooper to abandon his new faith. At the place of execution he was offered a box containing a pardon on condition that he recant. Hooper, characteristically, used the box as a step to climb on the pyre in which he would burn. His execution took place just to the west of the cathedral, between the college gate and the church of St Mary de Lode. Visitors today are probably misled by what they see. It is a quiet spot, and the statue of Hooper that stands there has him wearing vestments he would never have tolerated. On the day of the burning, 9 February 1555, the place was thronged; spectators hung from the branches of trees and crowded the windows round about. The queen's order spelt out his fate:

> Whereas, JOHN HOOPER, who of late was called Bishop of Worcester and Gloucester, is by due order of the laws ecclesiastic condemned and judged for a most obstinate, false, detestable heretic, and committed to our secular power to be burned according to the wholesome and good laws of our realm …

It was an official death and it was brutal in the extreme (fig. 56). They bungled the fire, using green wood that would not burn. Then the wind put the fire out altogether, and poor Hooper had to urge

Fig. 56
Bishop Hooper's execution from Foxe's *Book of Martyrs*. The details are inaccurate.

them to do better: 'For God's love, good people, let me have more fire.' At last he died praying, 'Lord Jesus have mercy upon me, Lord Jesus receive my spirit.' The cathedral clergy were forced to watch from a building near by (fig. 58).

Altars restored

Queen Mary survived Bishop Hooper by three and a half years. Scholars now suggest that, had she lived, the convictions of men like Hooper would have been driven out of England permanently. As it was, Mary was succeeded by her Protestant sister Elizabeth I (1558–1603), and once again the community was in turmoil. James Brookes, Mary's bishop, had also died. William Jennings, the first dean of Gloucester, was still in post but suffering 'infirmity of his limbs'. For a time Gloucester was rudderless. It took Elizabeth nearly three years to appoint a new bishop, Richard Cheyney. Meanwhile Jennings was replaced, first by a man called Cooper and then by the austere, scholarly and largely absent figure of Laurence

Fig. 57
Queen Mary I (1554, oil on panel) by Antonio Moro, Prado, Madrid.

Fig. 59
Memorial to Thomas
and Christian Machen
and their children, 1614,
north aisle.

Fig. 60
Portrait of William Laud
in episcopal dress,
Church House,
Gloucester.

Fig. 58
St Mary's gate to the
west of the cathedral.
From these windows the
cathedral clergy
watched Hooper burn.

Humphrey, who clearly found his professorship in
Oxford a more stimulating challenge. These were not
great days for the cathedral; financial affairs were in a
muddle, there were mutterings about corruption,
and the fabric was not in good repair. The great
abbey had fallen on hard times, and, it seems, those
responsible for its life were not eager to set their
house in order. The dean and chapter refused to co-
operate with the archbishop's officers, and when a
new dean was finally appointed there was an
unedifying argument about whether the statutes of
the cathedral had to be taken seriously. Protestant
services, using a revised Book of Common Prayer,
returned, but these were cautious times, when
religious conviction was more often expressed
through hatred of all things Roman rather than
through devotion and prayer.

When Queen Elizabeth died, problems in the
cathedral were dwarfed by the bigger concerns of the
city. Plague had broken out in 1603 and cut a swathe
through a city already impoverished and full of the
unemployed. It returned again and again. Business
prospered in other parts of the county but not in the
county town, and as the city fathers ran up debts they
began to complain about the government and taxation.
More damaging for relations with London, Gloucester
had become a Puritan city, where they paid to have
their own godly lecturer to tell them what scripture
really said, and rumours began to reach them of a
creeping fashionable popery around the royal court

Fig. 61
Memorial to Elizabeth Williams, daughter of Miles Smith, Lady Chapel.

(fig. 59). When Elizabeth's successor, James I, died in 1625, the knowledge that the new king, Charles I, had a popish wife stuck in Gloucester throats.

It was to this city that William Laud came as dean (fig. 60). The son of a Reading clothier, Laud was a man of great talent and even greater ambition. A meteoric career at Oxford culminated in his becoming president of St John's College in 1611, but he was still hungry for more success. He hung about the royal court and made some powerful friends. King James had his doubts about Laud but, in 1616, made him dean of Gloucester. It was a sop to all that ambition, but it probably did not pay to inspect this gift horse too closely. Years later Laud remarked, somewhat ruefully, that the king 'was pleased to say: He had given me nothing but Gloucester, which he well knew was a shell without a kernel'.

By January 1617 Laud was in Gloucester. It rapidly became clear to his new colleagues that their dean was a man in a hurry. Looking around, he found plenty of work to be done. However, his first act was a curious one: not a scheme of repair but seemingly a bit of religious housekeeping. The 'Chapter Acts

Book' solemnly records that the new dean ordered that 'The Communion Table should be placed altar wise' at the east end of the quire and railed off. The rails survive. No longer in the quire, they fence off the sanctuary in the Lady Chapel and still make a powerful statement about holy space and the barriers needed to preserve it (see fig. 45). Laud was being breathtakingly provocative. Altars had been moved from the east wall of churches in the time of Edward VI. They had been dragged forwards and turned through ninety degrees, which made the point that they were not altars at all but tables. Protestant, Prayer Book using congregations gathered round these tables, which were physical reminders of the fact that there were now no Catholic Masses in the English Church. Moving the table was not a bit of housekeeping after all; it was a statement about Reformation. Laud's altar declared defiantly that he was not ashamed of the Catholic past. He knew scripture and doctrine, but he also had new and unfamiliar interests; he believed in decency and reverence. He instructed the choir men to bow to his altar when they came in. Suddenly, the cathedral was

Fig. 62
Memorial to Margery
Clent , daughter of Miles
Smith, Lady Chapel.

not merely a Protestant church where you listened to the word of God; it had become a place where you worshipped with body and mind.

This was not an age of conciliation and compromise. Laud did not believe in tolerance or the middle way, and neither did his enemies. Chief among Laud's opponents was Miles Smith, bishop of Gloucester (1612–24). Smith was a convinced Protestant, the sort of person we might call 'Puritan'. He was also a distinguished scholar, who had translated scripture for the new Authorised Version of the Bible, published in 1611, and had been invited to write its preface. There was a row. The local clergy and some of the townspeople were outraged, the bishop's chaplain complained, and the canons disagreed among themselves. Smith threatened his new dean but instantly had to step back. Laud had told the king that Gloucester was in turmoil and hinted that the bishop could not keep his house in order. The king wanted the fighting to stop, and the bishop knew that he was beaten. Both the altar and the rails remained. The story goes that Smith never stepped inside the cathedral again, but that was a bit of malice spread years later, when Laud was put on trial. Smith, in truth, was rather mild-mannered and remembered here best as the father of the two tragic figures commemorated by striking tombs in the Lady Chapel, both of whom died in childbirth (figs 61 and 62).

The new dean moved on to other challenges: beginning repairs, sorting out the archive and reinstating morning prayer, in the Lady Chapel, at six o'clock. He also set about raising the standard of music by having work done on the organ and harassing the singing men into better behaviour. The 'Chapter Acts Book' records a sorry catalogue of punishments for drunkenness and fighting. Rowland Smith, who was admitted a lay clerk in 1618, was the worst offender. After a series of other offences, he attacked a city serjeant with a knife. Laud brought his days in the choir to a rapid conclusion.

Fig. 63
Memorial to Abraham
and Gertrude
Blackleech, south
transept.

In 1621 Laud's ambition carried him off to St David's to be bishop. From there he would move ultimately to Lambeth, as archbishop of Canterbury, and, as the country plunged into civil war, to a trial and to the scaffold. After his departure, life in Gloucester was a little less bad-tempered, but the arguments continued nonetheless. In 1625 a new bishop was enthroned. Godfrey Goodman, like Laud, was a high churchman and gave new silver plate to the cathedral. Six years later there was a more significant change, when Accepted Frewen was made dean (1631–44). He too was an ally of Laud, and the two worked together to introduce more of the beauty of holiness into what had been such a starkly Protestant building. Cushions and hangings brought colour back within all that scrubbed and scraped stonework.

At this stage the minor canons and lay clerks were housed in an appalling set of hovels on the north side of the cathedral that rejoiced under the name of 'Babylon'. The building and the morality of what went on there were swiftly reformed. Meanwhile the singing men were kept busy. An inventory of music books from 1641 tells us that they were singing the music of Richard Dering, Giovanni Coperario and William Lawes, as well as works by Jenkins, Simpson and Ives. It is likely they also knew and used music by Byrd, Tallis, Mundy, Morley and, later, Weelkes, Gibbons, Batten and Tomkins.

Now that silks and velvet adorned the cathedral and gilt flagons and plate stood on the altar, old divisions between townspeople and the cathedral community hardened into outright hostility. Two early seventeenth-century tombs illustrate this. The first, in the north aisle, offers a glimpse of the disciplined and rather dour faith of the city fathers: to this day the puritan physician John Bowyer still casts a bleak eye over choirs and clergy who stand, robed before a service, under the inscription on his tomb, Vayne Vanytie, All is but Vayne. A tomb in the

Fig. 64
A bird of prey at the feet
of Abraham Blackleech
– a detail from the tomb.

south transept commemorates Abraham Blackleech, a benefactor who had a lease on a property at the east end of the cathedral. It was erected in 1639 and suggests a more flamboyant kind of piety (figs 63 and 64). Opinion was hardening like stone.

The siege of Gloucester

As tension mounted, a Protestant Parliament turned on the king and his advisers, and religion was one of their chief complaints. The Root and Branch Bill, pressing reform, was debated in 1641 and received strong support from Thomas Pury, a Gloucester MP who urged, in particular, the abolition of deans and chapters. He read aloud in the House of Commons from the statutes of Henry VIII, no doubt rolling his eyes as he listed the duties cathedral clergy should perform: 'to keep residence, feed the poor, distribute alms, preach the word of God, have the youth profitably taught and keep a common table.' Pury complained: 'It is notoriously knowne to the city of Gloucester and country there abouts, That not one of the said Statutes before mentioned, are, or ever were, during my remembrance kept…' He proposed a scheme to turn the cathedral into a parish church with a group of preaching ministers. He did not get his way, but a new and much more Protestant broom was sweeping away all the ornaments that Laud had

introduced. By 1642 the organ and the choir had been abolished (fig. 65). Two years later communion tables across the country were moved away from the east end; tapers, altar rails, crucifixes and all pictures were removed. Once again the beauty of holiness was brought low.

Gloucester was briefly at the heart of the Civil War. Royalist successes at Exeter and Bristol were followed by a siege of the city in August and September 1643. It is said that the cathedral did not suffer during the siege, in part because it was protected by woolsacks but also because King Charles gave orders that it was not to be bombarded. Even so, we know that musket fire was directed at the tower. Parliament, recognising the importance of Gloucester, sent the earl of Essex to relieve the city. He raised the siege on 5 September 1643, a day that quickly became 'Gloucester Holiday'. It felt like good news in the city, but it was not good news for the cathedral. More damage was done after the siege than during it. The cloisters became stables, there was vandalism in the Lady Chapel, and the monument to Robert of Normandy was torn to pieces. These were the last, dying days of what Laud had created. Accepted Frewen fled, first to Oxford and then to France, 'until the fury of the times abated'. Parliament ejected the rest of the clergy, and poor Bishop Goodman learned that his enemies had, with startling energy and efficiency, plundered all five of his houses. His papers and books were scattered, and his wealth destroyed. He died, a broken man, in January 1656.

Cathedrals and their clergy had no place in the New Jerusalem that Parliament wanted to build. Cathedral rents were sequestered, and trustees appointed to manage them. In August 1644 that income was directed to pay £100 each year to an 'orthodox preacher' for a weekly sermon in the cathedral, with a further £50 to a preacher for a city church. In June 1645 Mr Jackson was appointed to the cathedral post, while the splendidly named Mr

Fig. 65
The Restoration organ
case, 1662, with the
smaller chaire organ of
1642 below.

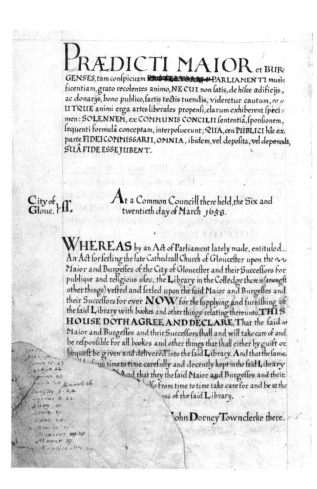

Fig. 66
Library Benefactions
Book showing the name
of the Town Clerk, John
Dorney.

Help-on-High Fox went to the church of St Nicholas.
The cathedral fell into poor repair, and the citizens of
Gloucester finally decided to pull it down. The roof
of the Lady Chapel had already suffered when ropes
and pulleys were set up to take down the cathedral
tower. Then John Dorney, the town clerk, appealed to
the city fathers to 'joyn your shoulders to hold up the
stately fabrick of the Colledge-Church (the great
ornament of this City)'. Dorney almost certainly
saved the cathedral and ought to be considered one
of its greatest benefactors. A scheme of repair was
begun, and Thomas Pury, son of the MP, stepped
forward to found a cathedral library. His generosity
is recorded in the beginning of the book used to
record gifts to the library (fig. 66):

> HE HIMSELF, animated by his enthusiasm and
> concern for learning both secular and divine,
> and lest an undertaking so extensive and of such
> importance should be left unfinished, FROM HIS
> OWN FORTUNE, as we understand, contributed
> what was lacking and so brought the unfinished
> work to a happy conclusion.

The library was in the chapter house (fig. 67), where
Pury's coat of arms can still be seen in the north side
of the east window. Thomas Pury senior gave a 1536
Coverdale Bible (see fig. 51), still in the library's
collection.

It was with this flourish in the cathedral that the
Commonwealth ended and Charles II returned from
exile. Instantly, the estates of bishops and cathedral
chapters were returned to the Church, and surviving
clergy were restored to their old jobs or to something
better. Accepted Frewen was one of the chief
beneficiaries and became archbishop of York. No
wonder there was a celebration in Gloucester, with a
bonfire on coronation day.

DAVID HOYLE

Fig. 67
The chapter house fitted
out as a library, from an
eighteenth-century
print by Thomas Bonnor,
1796.

CATHEDRAL AND COMMUNITY

A NEW BISHOP OF GLOUCESTER, William Nicholson, was consecrated on 6 January 1661, and the liturgy of the Prayer Book – forbidden for so long – was reinstated. As the see was not a particularly rich one, however, the bishop was permitted to hold other offices in plurality. William Brough, the dean, had been installed many years earlier, in November 1644, though it was not until August 1660 that he was finally able to take up his appointment. Sixteen years as dean-in-waiting must surely be some kind of record. It is noted that he was also granted the rectory of Beverston to augment his stipend. But if life was to return to normality, it required more than a dean and chapter in residence at the cathedral.

The Restoration of Charles II

The years of the Commonwealth had been turbulent and unhappy ones for the cathedral. A gaping hole in the cathedral accounts marks this period. The 'Chapter Acts Book' shows the broad range of matters with which the dean and prebendaries had to deal. The appointments of cathedral officers, servants and almsmen and the admission of singing men and boys were all recorded, as well as matters relating to the property and management of the estates. The chapter's accounts begin again in 1660, but they were in complete disarray. There were numerous lawsuits, which the chapter launched in an attempt to claw back land and property that had been purchased by Puritans. Their reluctance to surrender these estates is well documented.

Trying to identify the various tenants and understand the complexities of individual leases was another daunting task facing the chapter's beleaguered treasurer, Hugh Naish. The poor man wrote a despairing note in his accounts in 1660 that 'the places of the Church Revenue not summed up in this yeares Account, were not charged on the present Treasurer because through the unsettlement of the times hee knewe not exactly what to demaunde'. In

Fig. 68
Historiated initial 'C' showing Charles II. From the charter accompanying the cathedral's sealed copy of the 1662 Book of Common Prayer.

Fig. 69
'Verger's Rodd', 1661, bearing the coat of arms of Charles II.

Fig. 70
Silver-gilt cup and flagon, both part of the cathedral communion plate commissioned in 1662.

fact, without the chapter seal – of which there was no trace – no chapter business could legally be conducted. It is likely that during the Civil War the seal had either been sent away for safe keeping or destroyed. Whatever its fate, a new one was hastily commissioned, depicting the Holy Trinity. The cost of this was £2 7s. 6d.

But by far the greatest problem facing the dean and chapter was the state of the cathedral building itself. It was in desperate need of repair and required urgent attention. The Gloucester city fathers were probably quite relieved that it was no longer their responsibility. There were, according to the records of the time, a healthy collection of workmen – carpenters, joiners, glaziers, plumbers, masons – engaged in the cathedral refurbishment, so that it was 'assiduously repaired and rebuilt'. The building was substantially renovated; this work included a

large number of windows being reglazed and several floors repaved. Over and above this, the cathedral had to be refurnished and equipped for the restored services. This required the purchase of such things as candles, bread and wine, printed music books and prayer books (fig. 68). In 1661, £6 9s. 6d. was paid for 'the Vergers Rodd'. This verge, with the coat of arms of Charles II stamped on it (fig. 69), is still used by the vergers today in procession. All of the old communion plate had disappeared; it is assumed this had been melted down for money to fund the Civil War. The records show that in 1662 a magnificent new set was acquired. An inventory of 1673 lists the new plate as: 'Two silver guilt Candlesticks; One large silver guilt Dish; Two silver guilt fflagons; Two silver guilt Cups with Covers; One silver guilt plate for Bread.' Some of this plate is on display in the treasury exhibition (fig. 70).

Important among the cathedral's property were the remaining manuscripts of the monastic library. At the Restoration, when the dean and chapter took back the cathedral and its property, they also took over ownership of the library. After the Civil War this had been re-established in the former monastic chapter house. The intention of the public-spirited men who had carried out the scheme was that the new library should be open to anyone who might benefit from using it. However, it now became very much the private library of the dean and chapter. From the Restoration until the late nineteenth century the chapter house was generally referred to as the 'college library'. Owing to the accumulation of books in the chapter house during that time, chapter meetings were held in a little room leading off the north transept by St Paul's Chapel, which today is the Song School.

Disputes between high and low churchmen still continued, and a number of colourful characters made their presence felt during the late seventeenth century. Bishop Nicholson, who had been a fearless champion of the Church during the Commonwealth, was bishop of the diocese from January 1661. In his 1664 Visitation articles he tried to enforce uniformity in worship throughout the diocese and to reform abuses in the parochial system. He insisted on the residence of the clergy and robustly enquired of them about the repair of the fabric, table and vessels such as paten, chalice and flagon. Dr Robert Frampton was dean of Gloucester in 1673 and then became bishop in 1681. When the reign of James II ended in the 'Glorious Revolution' of 1688 and the Protestant William of Orange and his wife, Mary, were crowned, Frampton refused to take the oath of allegiance. As a result of this action, he was deprived of his bishopric.

One example of a clash of temperaments occurred in 1679, between prebendaries Gregory and Fowler, over the destruction of medieval glass in the west window of the quire. The two men could not have been more different in temperament or in their religious and political convictions. This stained glass bore a traditional representation of the Trinity: God the Father as an old man, God the Son as a crucifix and God the Holy Spirit as a dove. Fowler, the low churchman, regarded it as idolatrous. At a somewhat unusual chapter meeting, held in the absence of the dean and without normal records being kept, Fowler obtained a majority agreement that it should be removed. Before anything further could be done, Fowler himself climbed on to the nave roof and smashed the 'scandalous' glass with a pole. One of the other prebends records: 'Mr ffowler hee it was yt with a long pole dasht it to peices, in ye sight of man, and some strangers of quality yn in ye church.' Gregory, a high churchman, objected vigorously to all this. Since he was unable to have his objections recorded in the 'Chapter Acts Book', he made sure his side of the story was noted by writing it in the 'Register of Leases'. Fowler went on to become incumbent of St Giles, Cripplegate, and was appointed bishop of Gloucester in 1691, after the accession of William and Mary. Mercifully for both men, Gregory had died some months before Fowler returned as bishop.

Musical life and the Three Choirs Festival

The reconstitution of the choral establishment was perhaps the most complex undertaking for the cathedral at the Restoration. Once a choir has been dispersed, it is difficult to revive it, and the cathedral had been without music for over seventeen years. In fact in 1660 no one younger than twenty-five would have had first-hand knowledge of the cathedral's ancient choral tradition. There is no surviving record of the appointment of an organist or master of the choristers during the Civil War or Commonwealth period. Fortunately for Gloucester, a number of lay clerks who were appointed before the

Fig. 71
The opening of an anthem by Purcell from an original bass part-book in the Library.

Commonwealth period resumed their appointments, filling some of the singing men's places; this was particularly valuable in terms of continuity with the earlier choral tradition. Newly appointed choristers must have found their first encounter with this unfamiliar music fairly daunting. Thanks to encouragement from the king, who supported the re-establishment of the choirs at his chapels royal, considerable amounts of new music and anthems were being written, so it was also an exciting time (fig. 71).

As part of the restoration of the cathedral services a new organ was thought to be necessary. There is a record of Robert Webb visiting Bristol in 1663, to be followed by a visit from a Bristol organ builder named Taynton, who was paid £10 by the dean and chapter of Gloucester for 'tuning and setting up the organ'. This was probably the old organ, which had been in use before the Restoration, since it was not until 26 October 1663 that the dean and chapter agreed to pay the Harris family for supplying a new organ. The records show a first payment of £40 'to Mr. Tho. Harris towards the new organ he is to make, this being pd at ye ensealinge of the Articles'. The account books enable the progress of the work to be followed and show that the craftsmen already employed in the cathedral did much of the structural work and probably the carving.

The entries for the payments to Harris, who received a total of about £400 for his work, and the sums received from those recorded as 'friends' are shown in a separate account for each of the years 1663–64, 1664–65 and 1665–66. The new organ was built in a loft above the quire stalls, under the arch between the quire and the south transept. Evidence of supports for the loft can be still be seen in the stonework, and a tracing by F. S. Waller of a painting (now lost) shows the quire with its early eighteenth-century woodwork, with the organ in this position.

A number of problems were involved with the repositioning of the organ; not all of them were mechanical ones. This is shown by the payment in December 1665 for 'A new box to keep the organ books from the Ratts: And allsoe a Trap to catch ye Ratts all this in ye organ Loft'. This is followed by a payment of 2s. 6d. on 17 November 1666 to 'Mr Jordan [an apothecary] for medicines for the rats that troubled the Organ Bellace [bellows?]'. There were also many payments in succeeding years to Thomas Harris for repairs to the organ. In 1674 the dean and chapter made an agreement with Thomas Harris and 'Rene Harris his sonne' that for a yearly sum of £5 they would 'well and sufficiently keepe the organ in as good repaire as it now is especially as to the musique part of it'.

By some kind of miracle the beautiful organ case, designed by Thomas Harris and completed in 1666, has escaped destruction and alteration. The case was made by local Gloucester craftsmen and incorporates the richly carved case of a chaire organ, which was probably the previous cathedral organ and dates from between 1630 and 1640. The re-gilding of the organ was carried out by John Campion, who also decorated the organ case and pipes. In no other English cathedral does a seventeenth-century double case survive in its original shape with unaltered display pipes and decoration of this quality and exuberance. Harris's organ continues to be used every day by the cathedral's director of music, his assistant and the organ scholar.

In 1718 William Hine, who was in charge of the music at the cathedral, organised the removal of the organ from beneath the south crossing arch to its central position over the west entrance of the quire (fig. 72). This was a bold and imaginative move, provoking considerable controversy at the time. It was Hine who brought a new professionalism to the musical life and choral tradition of the cathedral and established new standards of excellence. About this time (possibly 1715) the annual music meeting of the three choirs of Hereford, Worcester and Gloucester cathedrals began. The Three Choirs Festival has continued annually, rotating from Gloucester to Worcester and Hereford; it has been interrupted only twice in its history, by the world wars of the twentieth century. Today it is the oldest surviving music festival in Europe.

Daniel Lyson's *History of the Music Meeting* (1812) records that the first annual Music Meeting to be advertised in the *Gloucester Journal* was in 1723, though the three choirs had been meeting annually for some years before that. The first Gloucester Music Meeting is recorded as taking place in 1721. The first recorded performance of music by Handel at the Three Choirs Festival appears in the *Gloucester Journal* of Tuesday 17 August 1736. A notice states that 'Mr Purcell's *Te Deum* will be performed on Wednesday morning, and Mr Handel's on the Thursday morning'. The Music Meetings (as they were originally referred to) had attendant attractions. They provided a focal point in the social calendar for the nobility, gentry, better-off clergy and any family whose head could lay claim to the title of 'gentleman'. Timed to follow the annual harvest, the meetings provided an interlude of civic hospitality in late August or September, before the more serious business of winter hunting began.

The cathedral in the age of reason

During the eighteenth century the Anglican Church became increasingly associated with the aristocracy and the gentry, and it was essentially supportive of their efforts at preserving the status quo. Fashions were changing; passionate convictions began to fade, and clergy and congregations held a more genteel faith. This was based on morality, reason and confidence in human enlightenment. There was broad satisfaction with the established social order, and the established ways of the Church.

Repairs to the cathedral were made over two main periods. While Dr Knightley Chetwood was dean (1707–20), he concentrated on refurbishing the quire (fig. 73). During this phase Abbot Wigmore's pulpitum was pulled down and the 'square stone pulpit' was destroyed, its place being taken by the organ. The Gloucester Corporation minutes of 1717 approve a present of £50 to the dean, as a contribution to his 'work of large expence by Beautifying and Enlarging the [Quire]' for the better accommodation of the Corporation and citizens and, specifically, for moving the organ.

The second period of major structural and decorative alterations to the cathedral was during the time of Bishop Martin Benson, who was largely responsible for the refurbishment of the nave and

Fig. 72
Thomas Harris's 1666 organ in its central position over the west entrance of the quire.

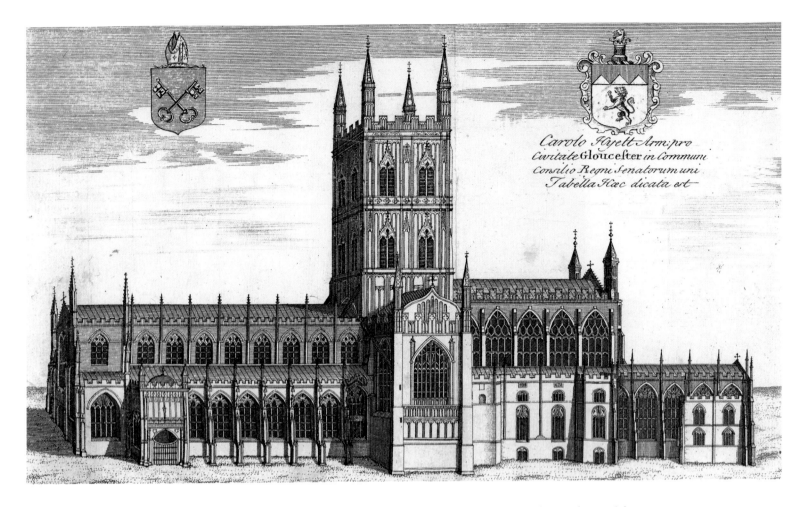

Carolo Hyett Arm: pro
Civitate Gloucester in Communi
Consilio Regni Senatorum uni
Tabella Hæc dicata est

Lady Chapel. He was bishop of Gloucester from 1734 until 1752 and refused translation to a better-endowed bishopric. He combined spirituality with sociability, and a fellow bishop wrote that 'his purity, though awfully strict, was inexpressibly amiable'. Bishop Benson believed that laughter and mirth were consistent with 'the religion of a good man'. He was respected both by establishment figures and by reformers. Even John Wesley referred to him as 'the good Bishop Benson'. This was quite an achievement since Wesley rarely paid people compliments.

It is possible that Martin Benson's family connections made him sympathetic to medieval architecture. He was descended through his paternal grandmother from Samuel Fell, dean of Christ Church, Oxford. Benson was also a cousin of the eccentric antiquary Browne Willis (1682–1760), who spent considerable sums of his own money restoring churches. Benson and his architect, William Kent, attempted to soften or lighten the medieval building.

Kent's decorated quire screen, with neoclassical form and Gothic features, was inserted at the east end of the nave in 1741 (fig. 74). Kent proposed that the massive nave pillars should be fluted, but he was deterred by fears that tampering with their ashlar facing might disturb their rubble core. The Georgian transformation of Gloucester Cathedral's nave proposed by Benson and Kent would not have been dissimilar to the Perpendicular remodelling begun by Abbot Morwent three centuries earlier.

In the Lady Chapel, Kent designed a stucco (plaster) decoration to cover the mutilated reredos behind the altar (fig. 75). It showed divine light radiating outwards and was perhaps a suitable symbol of the age of Enlightenment. During the later Georgian period damage occurred in the Lady Chapel. In June 1798 it is reported in the chapter records that 'a quantity of painted glass has been largely stolen from the East Window of the Cathedral'. (Because the Lady Chapel's east window is far more

Fig. 73
Exterior view of the cathedral, c.1710, during Dean Knightley Chetwood's alterations to the quire.

Fig. 74
Drawing of the nave by Thomas Bonnor, 1796. William Kent's screen, 1741, and memorials on the Norman piers can be seen.

Fig. 75
Thomas Bonnor's view of Lady Chapel, 1796, showing William Kent's 'Radiance' behind the altar.

Fig. 77
Mayor's seat in the quire, ordered in 1738 by the chapter.

Fig. 76
Detail from the restored east window of the Lady Chapel, in which medieval glass has been reused.

accessible than the Great East Window of the cathedral it is likely that the chapter records are slightly ambiguous.) A reward of 50 guineas was offered to help catch the culprits; the size of the reward indicates that a large quantity of medieval glass was taken. It is almost certain that this theft precipitated the restoration and present arrangement of the medieval glass in the Lady Chapel window (fig. 76).

Bishop Benson was also responsible for renewing

the paving of the nave. This was an expensive and
necessary work, but the bishop managed to turn the
failings of members of the chapter to the benefit of
the fabric. Any fines he levied on the canons when
they failed to fulfil their due terms of residence were
spent on repairs. Few of Bishop Benson's
contributions to the cathedral survive today. The
screen was replaced by another (more purely Gothic)
design in 1820, and the plasterwork on the Lady
Chapel reredos was removed in 1819. His fine
monument is in the south tribune gallery, banished
from its original place in the south transept. Only a
modest tablet in his memory survives on the west
wall of the nave north aisle. He was a generous
patron of the cathedral, and it is sad to note that little
of his contribution to its restoration has survived.
One important item from that era still in use today is
the mayor's seat in the quire (fig. 77). This was
ordered in 1738 by the chapter, to persuade the
mayor and corporation to attend the cathedral
instead of St Nicholas's Church in Westgate Street.

The cathedral precincts

After the restoration of the monarchy, the Cathedral
Close, largely unaltered since medieval times, was
about to change. Fine buildings began to appear in
various parts of the city, including the cathedral
precincts, which reflected the growing affluence of
the merchant classes. In the 1660s new leases were
granted to a number of the buildings, which resulted
in large amounts of restoration and alteration.

The remains of the old monastic infirmary, an area
which had become known as 'Babylon', had been
subdivided and extended to provide accommodation
for the families of servants of the cathedral (fig. 78).
This was chronically overcrowded; its inhabitants
were sundry assorted widows, minor canons, lay
clerks and others. At this time changes began to take
place, which made this part of the Close 'less
unsavoury' than it had previously been. It was here
that John Stafford Smith, composer of the American
national anthem, was born in 1750. He was the son
of a long-serving cathedral organist, Martin Smith.

John was christened in Gloucester Cathedral, educated at the cathedral school and became an accomplished choirboy.

In the former monastic Inner Court, which is known as Millers Green, there is a tall house, known as 'No. 1', built around 1740. It has an impressive pedimented stone doorway, and the forecourt has gate piers with handsome urns and wrought-iron railings. This property became the Deanery in 1940. Previous deans had occupied Church House, formerly the prior's lodgings, at the north-west corner of the cathedral. Another house, 7 Millers Green, was built about 1670 on the site of the western end of the Parliament Room, which had been destroyed some centuries earlier by a substantial fire. A blue plaque affixed to the front of the house records the fact that it was the home of the celebrated organist and composer S. S. Wesley, grandson of the great John Wesley, while he was cathedral organist. In fact, he died in one of the ground-floor rooms. The tall elegant house that is 6 Millers Green and known as 'Queen Anne House' was built in 1680 (fig. 79).

One of the most impressive houses in the Cathedral Close is 9 College Green (fig. 80). It was built around 1707 by Samuel Ricketts on a site formerly occupied by the abbey stables and dunghill. It has three storeys and an imposing entrance. One of its more interesting inhabitants was the eccentric widow, Mrs Frances Cotton, who occupied the house in 1753. She kept a small aviary containing a robin in her pew near the high altar of the cathedral. Mrs Cotton believed that the little bird was the reincarnation of her favourite daughter, who had died some years earlier. Sir Horace Walpole commented: 'The chapter indulge this whim as she contributes abundantly to glaze, white wash and ornament the church.' In the 1770s, 9 College Green was let to Dr John Wall, whose father was the founder of the Worcester china factory.

Along the west wall of College Green, on the site

Fig. 79
View of Miller's Green showing Queen Anne House, built in 1680, and the Parliament Room.

Fig. 80
No. 9 College Green,
built in 1707, by Samuel
Ricketts.

of the old monastic stabling, four houses were built. 12 College Green(formerly Beaufort House), which now houses the cathedral office, was built in 1737 by Alderman Benjamin Saunders, an affluent wine merchant and owner of the King's Head Inn in Westgate Street. In this house he established a 'Great Room' for the holding of dances and assemblies. The building also served as a coffee house and a venue for music recitals and public breakfasts. It is recorded that guests could play battledore and shuttlecock to the accompaniment of a band playing appropriate music. The row of houses on the south side of Upper Green were rebuilt between 1750 and 1760, and 6 College Green, the former sexton's house, adjacent to King Edward's Gate, was enlarged and extended in 1813 by adding spacious Georgian rooms.

In the early eighteenth century there began an interesting and unusual connection between Oxford University and Gloucester Cathedral. This was the appointment of a prebend to the fifth stall who also held the mastership of Pembroke College, Oxford. This was instituted in November 1718, to augment his meagre stipend. As a canon of Gloucester, the master of Pembroke also had a house within the precincts. At first the house adjoining St Mary's Gate (Monument House) was assigned to him, but from the early nineteenth century he occupied the house now known as King's School House. This had grown from a small dwelling on the former monastic Common Orchard to a spacious Georgian residence. The master of Pembroke came to Gloucester 'in residence' during July, August or September (the summer vacation). The arrangement was convenient not only to the holder of the office, in providing him with a summer 'seat', but also to the cathedral. It was noted that the tone of the chapter meetings was raised and that other members of the chapter 'benefited enormously' from having the master of Pembroke with them during the summer. This arrangement continued until 1937.

Fig. 81
Memorial to Judge John
Powell, 1713, Lady
Chapel.

People of Gloucester Cathedral and city

In the eighteenth century a number of elegant town houses were built in the city. Two of these, Bearland House and Ladybellgate House, were the homes of the Raikes family. Robert, the founder of the Sunday School movement, was born in 1736 in Ladybellgate House; his father had begun the local newspaper *The Gloucester Journal* in 1722. When Robert took over its production, he used this to raise public awareness of the state of the poor, the harsh treatment of prisoners and the need for proper schooling for children. With the Revd Thomas Stock he started the Sunday school movement. There is a memorial to Stock in the south aisle of the cathedral, near to a memorial to the Revd Richard Raikes, Robert's brother.

Josiah Tucker, dean of Gloucester (1758–99), was a highly regarded economist and theologian. He carried out extensive improvements to the cathedral precincts and to the management of its estates. There is a memorial tablet extolling Dean Tucker's virtues and achievements on the east wall of the south transept. His congregation included the eccentric (and aforementioned) Mrs Cotton.

Judge John Powell's memorial in the Lady Chapel is unmissable (fig. 81). Powell was born in 1645 and died in 1713. He was, in his time, a barrister, judge, MP, sheriff, mayor and town clerk of Gloucester. He was appointed to the bench in 1686 and knighted in 1687. Although he looks severe in effigy, he was described by Dean Swift as 'an old fellow with grey hairs who was the merriest old gentleman I ever saw who spoke pleasing things and chuckled until he cried'. During his time as a judge, the law relating to witchcraft had not been repealed, although to a large extent the voracity of witch-hunting had abated. Judge Powell conducted the last trial for witchcraft in England in 1712. A certain Jane Wenman had been taken into custody following sworn statements that she could fly. The judge asked her if the allegations were true. The accused replied that she could indeed fly, to which the

Fig. 82
Memorial to Sarah
Morley carved by John
Flaxman, 1784, north
aisle.

judge smilingly responded 'So you may, if you will, for I have no law against flying' and promptly dismissed the case. He is said to have laughed the courts out of the Middle Ages and into the age of reason. His memorial in the Lady Chapel is by Thomas Green of Camberwell, and Judge Powell's name is recorded on a ledger stone near by. The memorial is the standing figure of the judge in white marble, dressed in the robes of a judge of the King's Bench.

Another beautiful monument is situated in the north aisle (fig. 82). Sarah Morley died in childbirth, aged twenty-eight, on board a ship returning from India in 1784. (Tragically, her sister died in the same

manner the same year; her memorial is in nearby Newent church.) Sarah's monument is carved by John Flaxman (also responsible for the tombs of Lord Nelson and Joshua Reynolds in St Paul's Cathedral). Sarah is shown rising from the sea with her babe on her left arm, being received amid clouds by three beautifully sculptured angels who are floating towards her. One grasps her by the hand, and another welcomes her, while the third points her heavenwards. The two roundels depict 'A Pelican in her Piety' (a symbol of self-sacrifice, as the pelican feeds her young with blood pecked from her own breast) and a dove mourning the death of its mate.

Fig. 83
Memorial to Sir George
Onesiphorous Paul
sculpted by R. W. Sievier,
1825, south aisle.

Fig. 84
Memorial to Dr Edward
Jenner sculpted by R. W.
Sievier, 1825, west end of
nave.

This magnificent memorial is carved in white marble on a background of black marble.

A memorial to another remarkable city worthy, found in the south aisle, is to Sir George Onesiphorous Paul (1746–1820; fig. 83). As high sheriff of Gloucester in 1781, Paul became aware of the deplorable conditions at the gaol. Paul worked for 'proof of criminality, against fetters and chains', and also for the provision of healthcare and separate accommodation for prisoners. His neoclassical monument is a robed bust on a large sarcophagus with clawed feet and large, free-standing base. Carved of white Carrara marble, it was sculpted by R. W. Sievier in 1825.

Dr Edward Jenner (1749–1823; fig. 84) was born in Berkeley and apprenticed at a young age to a surgeon. He developed the practice of vaccination with the live smallpox virus, to immunise against the disease. He struggled to make his technique widely known and suffered financially. His monument, a standing figure in white Carrara marble, was carved by Sievier in the same year as the Paul monument. Situated at the far west end of the nave, the figure of Jenner is shown wearing an academic gown and carrying a mortarboard in his left hand. One of his coat buttons is missing or undone, and no one knows why.

For those who have a passion for bells, the memorials to the Rudhall family at the west end of the north aisle near the entrance to the cloisters are worthy of inspection. The mural at the top is the oldest; it is to Elizabeth (d. 1699) and Abraham (d. 1736) Rudhall. Abraham was the founder of a bell foundry in Gloucester in 1684. This foundry remained in the family until 1828, when it was taken over by the Whitechapel foundry of London, which continues in business today. The Rudhall foundry made over 500 bells for churches in the county; more bells were sold and transported across the country by river and canal, and some were exported to the United States. All of the foundry's bells were stamped with a little bell and the Rudhall family initials. Over 4,000 bells were cast by the family, but the only complete ring of eight bells cast by one member, Abel, hangs in the Old North Church, Boston, Massachusetts. Many members of the Rudhall family are buried in the cloisters.

A number of more ancient memorials were defaced during the eighteenth century, among them two of the most significant in the cathedral. That of Abbot Parker, whose chantry chapel is situated in the north ambulatory, bears much graffiti and mutilation; the face is battered, and the nose missing. The stunning tomb and effigy of Edward II was robbed of many jewels and sustained superficial

damage, the alleged result of unruly behaviour by the pupils of the College School (now King's School) and choirboys (fig. 85).

During a period of almost 200 years, from the 1660s to the 1830s, the cathedral itself survived the comings and goings of no fewer than seventeen bishops and thirteen deans, some more illustrious than others. As the Georgian era came to an end, the cathedral was due to experience more dramatic changes over the ensuing fifty years than it had done over the preceding two centuries.

FRANCES KAY

Fig. 85
Detail from the alabaster effigy of Edward II in the north ambulatory, showing signs of mutilation and graffiti.

THE VICTORIAN REORDERING

THE FIRST HALF OF THE nineteenth century saw profound changes in English society. Industrialisation resulted in the rapid growth of towns and cities, and the development of railways from the 1840s encouraged the building of suburbs for the growing middle classes. At the same time the Evangelical and Oxford movements were bringing a renewed vision to the Church of England. Many new churches were built, generally in the Gothic style, and existing ones were restored or rebuilt. The work of A. W. Pugin was an inspiration to those who were to work on Gloucester Cathedral, as well as many other nineteenth-century architects and designers.

F. S. Waller and the 1855 report

Since the Reformation, other than necessary routine maintenance, little had been done to the fabric of the cathedral, the main focus of interest being the internal furnishings. In 1846 the British Archaeological Association met in Gloucester, and the architect George Godwin noted of the state of the cathedral that 'unless some proper supervision was exercised and some professional architect occasionally consulted, hereafter considerable expense would be entailed which might now be saved'. It seems the warning was heeded, and in 1855 the dean and chapter commissioned from the firm of Fulljames & Waller a survey of the fabric 'in order to place the Cathedral in as perfect a state as practicable'.

In 1839 Thomas Fulljames, in practice probably since 1830, had taken on as a pupil the seventeen-year-old Frederick Sandham Waller. In 1846 Waller became Fulljames's partner, and in 1852 he was appointed supervisor of works at the cathedral. Apart from a break following a riding accident in 1863, he served the cathedral in that capacity and as architect until 1905. In turn he was succeeded by his son F. W. Waller and his grandson N. H. Waller, who retired in 1960. Their influence on the restoration and conservation of the fabric and on the internal furnishings of the cathedral was considerable.

In the introduction to the 1855 report to the dean and chapter Waller stated: 'The general principle kept in view throughout is to retain in all cases as much as possible of the old work, restoring only where actually perished.' This philosophy of conservation and sympathetic restoration has been maintained ever since. (It was, however, to be frequently tested. As early as 1863 Fulljames was advising that a proposal to remove the perpendicular tracery of the north aisle windows and restore them to their supposed Norman originals was 'entirely opposed to the principle laid down in 1855 by Mr Waller'.) In the report the condition of the fabric and furnishings of each area of the cathedral was noted in detail, and proposals were made for 'alteration or restoration'. Waller set out what was to be the programme of work for the next fifty years, costed at £66,235 (equivalent to about £5 million today). The work was listed in order of priority: drainage and soil removal (much of which had already been done since 1846), the Great East Window, the north aisle roof and other roofs, external stonework and internal decoration.

Waller fortunately recognised the importance of the Great East Window: '[It] is sufficiently perfect to be interpreted. [It] is in a sad state of repair, the ironwork is in many parts eaten through and the glass retained in its place by mortar only. It is on this account that it is recommended as one of the first things to be attended to.' In 1860 the chapter decided to take the advice of the stained-glass expert Charles Winston on the restoration of the window. To him we probably owe the survival of this medieval masterpiece; twenty years later Waller was to describe Winston justifiably as 'an excellent man in advance of his time'. Winston was critical of some aspects of the window; for example, writing in 1863 in the *Archaeological Journal*, he stated 'the figures are ill-drawn, ungraceful and insipid'. He was clear,

Fig. 86
The quire in 1849, showing the new stone pulpit (1848) and the pews, benches and reredos later removed in George Gilbert Scott's restoration and reordering (1869–73).

OVERLEAF:
Fig. 87
The quire, with pavement (1873) and sub-stalls (1869–71), results of Gilbert Scott's restoration.

however, that there should be conservation rather than restoration, stating that 'the introduction of so much new glass' would 'have completely changed the general aspect of the window'. He advised the chapter not to accept the proposals of some firms of glass painters to replace the glass, including one (probably Wailes of Newcastle) for 'filling the entire window with rich glass'. Winston supervised the conservation and re-leading of the glass, which was back in place by the end of 1862 (see fig. 30). At the same time much of the stonework of the window and of the east end generally was replaced, more being necessary than had at first been anticipated.

The library had served as a schoolroom until it was damaged in 1849 by fire, supposedly started by the boys. The building of a new schoolroom on the site of the monastic dormitory meant that the library could be returned to its medieval function. Between 1856 and 1857 the fine timber roof was restored and a new floor laid, bookcases were moved from the old library and new ones made. These changes meant

that the chapter house, which had served as a library since the mid-seventeenth century, could be returned to its original purpose. The building was re-roofed, stonework repaired, lime wash (as elsewhere in the cathedral) cleaned off and a new floor of Minton tiles laid.

Most of the other work completed by 1863 was in the nave. Earlier, between 1848 and 1852, the west front had been restored, and this continued with the installation of the new west window in 1859 (see fig. 96). External stonework was repaired on both aisles, with one bay on the south side being restored, its newly cut ballflowers being seen as an exemplar for future work. The north aisle was re-roofed. Internally lime wash was cleaned from the nave and aisles, and memorials on the nave piers were removed.

Waller had also recommended that the nave floor be relaid with tiles 'adopting the old arrangement and pattern'; this was not achieved. Nevertheless, when forced into temporary retirement by his accident, Waller could justifiably be pleased with the

Fig. 88
The quire vault (c.1350), painted by Clayton & Bell (1870–71).

amount and quality of conservation and restoration achieved. Much, however, remained to be done, especially in the quire. For two years, until his retirement in 1865, Fulljames took over. The chapter then appointed George Gilbert Scott as architect.

George Gilbert Scott's transformation of the quire

Scott was perhaps the greatest of mid-Victorian architects. Although generally seen as a restorer rather than a conservator, he served Gloucester well. In 1855 his comments on Waller's report had been sought, and now he was asked to reconsider those plans, especially for the quire and Lady Chapel (fig. 86). Scott reported to the chapter in April 1867. He disagreed with Waller's proposals to transfer the organ to within the north transept crossing and to remove the screen between quire and nave; the latter

Fig. 90
David bringing the Ark from the house of Obededom, one of the intaglio scenes set in the presbytery pavement, 1873.

would have destroyed the medieval ordering of the quire and removed all but two of the medieval return stalls. However, he endorsed most of Waller's other proposals, for stalls, floor, sedilia and cleaning in the quire, and for glazing and removal of lime wash in the Lady Chapel. Interestingly, the cathedral archives record that both believed the badly damaged Lady Chapel reredos should be left 'without any attempt at its restoration' (Scott), 'the remains of the painting being so interesting and uncommon' (Waller).

On 5 December 1868 the *Gloucestershire Chronicle* was 'gratified to announce' that the restoration of the quire was about to begin. Arrangements had been made for services: 'The choir and transepts will be boarded off the grand old nave … the communion table will be placed against the organ screen … chairs will be provided and gas will be introduced.' When the lime wash was removed from the quire vault, no traces of medieval painting were found. Clayton & Bell were asked to prepare designs for polychrome

Fig. 89
Finial on the end of a quire sub-stall, 1869–71.

Fig. 91
George Gilbert Scott's
high altar reredos, 1873.

decoration, and once the chapter was satisfied with the sample provided, permission was given in 1870 for the work to proceed; as often happened, within a year they were being asked for funding additional to the contract (fig. 88).

The quire floor was a mixture of medieval tiles and stone slabs. The former survived particularly well in the sanctuary, and this fifteenth-century pavement was conserved, missing tiles being replaced by ones from elsewhere. The remainder of the quire was paved with new tiles, many with reproductions of medieval designs, made by Godwin of Lugwardine and completed in 1873 (fig. 87). In the presbytery eighteen black-and-white intaglio Old Testament scenes, designed by Scott, were set in the tiles (fig. 90). As so often with new work, opinions varied; H. J. L. J. Masse, in his *Bell's Guide* of 1899, wrote of 'the crudity and tastelessness of the pavement'.

The monastic rear stalls were cleaned and repaired, as were the misericords; fourteen new ones were cut. The eighteenth-century pews were removed and replaced in 1869–71 by the mayor's stall, bishop's *cathedra* and two rows of sub-stalls, notable for the beautifully carved ends and finials (fig. 89).

Waller had proposed restoring the high altar reredos to its 'former state'. Scott's design, completed in 1873, certainly derived much of its architectural detail from fourteenth-century work in the quire and especially from the tomb of Edward II. The carving was the work of Farmer & Brindley (also responsible for the new stalls). The figures were cut by J. F. Redfern, the main scenes being the Ascension, the Nativity and the Entombment. The reredos was painted by Clayton & Bell in 1888, but the figures within it were coloured only in 1963, by Dykes Bower (figs 91 and 92).

In 1872 Scott turned to the late medieval sedilia, of which mutilated canopies remained, with three angels on the parapet playing tabor and trumpets. Within the restored canopies were placed figures by Redfern of medieval abbots.

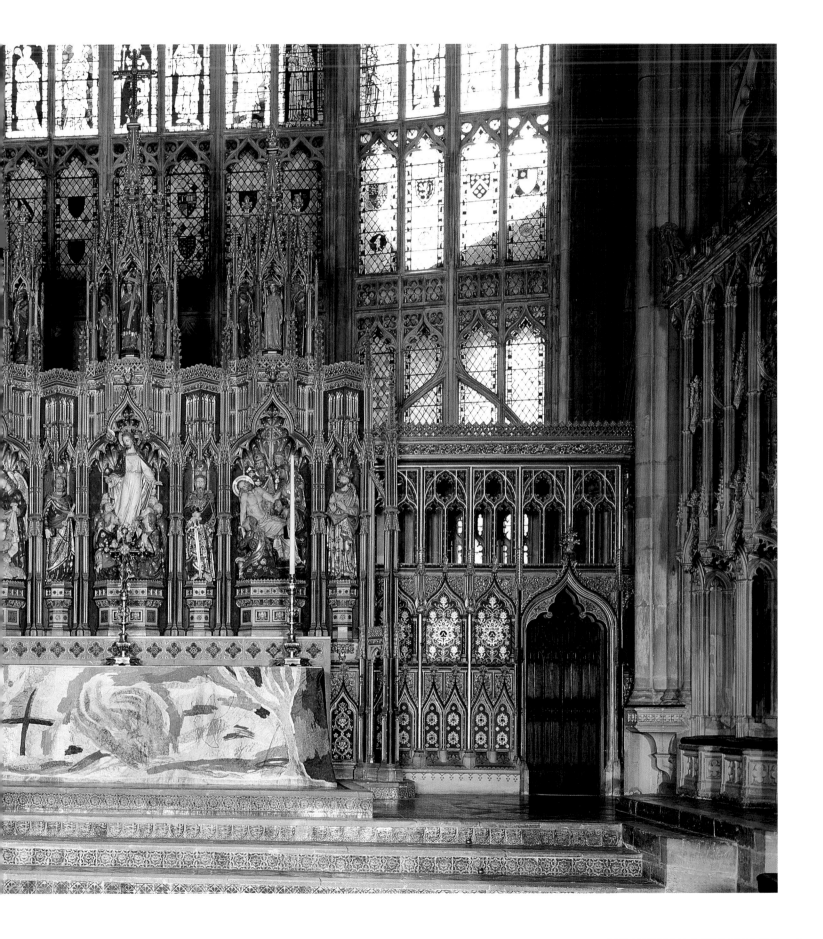

Elsewhere in the quire a new lectern, valued at £250, was given in 1866; the *Illustrated London News* noted the donor as Mr J. C. Dent of Sudeley Castle. Designed by J. F. Bentley and made by Hart & Son, it had been shown at the 1862 International Exhibition in London. Exhibited again at the Victoria and Albert Museum (1971–72), the catalogue states 'the magnificently formalized group of eagle and dragon represents the Gospel triumphing over Infidelity' (fig. 93). Less pleasing, perhaps, was Scott's font, of Norman design and carved in Aberdeen granite. Dedicated in 1878, it was placed originally at the west end of the nave; it is now in the crypt.

The south porch was also restored during this period. Some repairs had been completed in 1852, and the porch west window was glazed in 1854 with stamped quarries from James Powell & Sons. However, Waller's report listed the major problems that remained. In 1863 restoration was agreed, but work did not start until 1868, by which time Waller appears to have been back at work, Scott noting that 'Mr Waller, now recovered, has helped me in respect of the porch'. (Less happily, when the quire reredos was being completed, under Scott's instructions, Waller interfered, and eventually the workmen 'thrust him out'.) By 1871 the work was complete, including the replacement of most external stone, the removal of the sundial and the installation in the newly restored niches of figures sculpted by Redfern (see fig. 40).

Fig. 92
Detail of the high altar reredos, showing Redfern's carving of the Ascension and of St Peter and St Paul; polychrome design by Dykes Bower, 1963.

Fig. 93
The quire lectern,
designed by J. F. Bentley
and made by Hart &
Son, 1862.

The Victorian glass revival

During the three centuries after the dissolution of the abbey much of the stained glass must have been damaged or destroyed. Nothing is known about the iconoclasm, especially of the reign of Edward VI and during the Civil War; the only recorded example was the later destruction in 1679 of the quire west window by a member of the chapter. Some glass was evidently stolen; an advertisement in the *Gloucester Chronicle* from 1798 offered a reward of 50 guineas for information about the 'evil-minded and wicked persons who have of late years stolen the painted glass from the windows of the cathedral' (see p. 74). Vandalism, which included the throwing of stones by schoolboys, also played its part. Perhaps more than anything else, general neglect and careless repairs resulted in the windows losing much of their original glass.

Nevertheless, a significant amount of medieval glass appears to have survived into the nineteenth century. John Carter's engravings of 1807 show, albeit in a stylised and suspiciously repetitive manner, stained glass filling the heads of lights and traceries of windows on the north side of the cathedral. In 1856 Waller noted in his *General Architectural Description of Gloucester Cathedral*: 'there are remains of painted glass in several of the windows of the Nave, Transepts and Lady Chapel, and in the Clerestory windows of the Quire.' Much of this disappeared during the major re-glazing programmes of the following forty years.

An important development had been the growing interest in all things Gothic. Since the late eighteenth century collectors had been buying stained glass, especially from the closed abbeys of revolutionary France, the Rhineland and the Low Countries, and installing it in their homes or in churches in which they had a special interest. With this came a growing academic and technical interest in medieval glass, seen in the designs and writings of

A. W. Pugin and others, and, later, in the work of Charles Winston. The latter was closely involved in attempts by leading glass manufacturers to rediscover the medieval techniques of glass-making, which were bearing fruit by the early 1860s. These developments must be viewed in the context of the growing influence of the Oxford movement and of the many church-building and restoration programmes. The number of workshops making stained glass grew rapidly. National census returns record those working in this field rising from three in 1831 to 531 in 1851.

In his report to the chapter in 1855 Waller had noted in every part of the cathedral the bad condition of the glazing, and his recommendation throughout was to fill the windows with 'painted glass'. Interestingly, in the light of the loss that eventually occurred, Waller suggested 'reusing the old painted glass where possible' (the west window) and 'completing the designs in accordance with the existing remains'.

Pugin had argued that monuments on church walls were 'blisters'. Perhaps influenced by this, the chapter decided to encourage those who wished to commemorate the dead to do so by giving a window rather than by buying a traditional monument. They

Fig. 96
The nave west
window, made by the
Newcastle workshop
of William Wailes,
1859.

also, very cleverly, stipulated that the donation should include the cost of restoring the stonework of the window.

Waller recorded that in the cloisters the carrel windows and the lower lights of the main windows were bricked up. In 1854 he had proposed 'the filling up of the Windows of the Great Cloister with painted glass', and by the time of his report action was already being taken. Dr Francis Jeune, the chapter treasurer, proposed a glazing scheme on the theme of man's redemption, starting in the south-east corner with the prophesies of Christ's birth, followed by the Annunciation and the Nativity, Christ's ministry, death and Resurrection and the life of the early church. Waller commented in 1856 that the scheme 'was originated with a view to check the disfigurement of the cathedral by monuments of any other description'.

Thus in 1854 permission was given for the installation half-way along the east walk of a window in memory of Dr Thomas Evans, the subject being the boy Jesus in the Temple (fig. 94). The manufacturer was John Hardman of Birmingham, originally makers of ecclesiastical metalwork but since 1845 producers of stained glass, especially for Pugin. The designer of this first figurative window to be installed in the cathedral since the Reformation was John Hardman Powell, Hardman's nephew and Pugin's son-in-law. By 1868 the glazing of the east walk had been completed, all but two windows (by Ballantine of Edinburgh and Clayton & Bell) coming from the Hardman studios. Except for one window in the north walk and two in the south walk, Dr Jeune's scheme remains unrealised.

In 1868 the cloister *lavatorium* was glazed, again by Hardman to Powell designs. The main lights, appropriately for the monastic washing area, illustrate episodes from Christ's ministry associated with water, the one exception being the lights furthest east, which depict creation (fig. 95). The glass is of the highest

Fig. 98
The crucifixion of St Andrew in the south transept chapel, painted in spirit fresco by Thomas Gambier Parry, 1866–68.

quality and among the finest in the cathedral.

No overall scheme was proposed for the nave, and donors seem to have had a free hand in choosing manufacturer and subject. Between 1858 and 1866 every window, with one exception, was filled with new glass or, in the case of two partly surviving fifteenth-century windows in the north aisle, carefully restored. This last work was that of Hardman & Co., also responsible for the Lucius Legend and the Justice windows towards the west end of the aisles. The large west window (fig. 96),

made by the Newcastle firm of William Wailes, has at its centre the Nativity, and above and below are incidents involving baptism and water. Impressive at a distance, close up the painting is of variable quality. (Dr H. D. Spence, dean from 1886 to 1917, wrote in 1913 of the earlier Victorian glass that much 'is regrettable and poor, of which the most conspicuous example is the great west window'.)

In the south aisle of the nave are two important windows from the major workshop of Clayton & Bell. One, from 1860, depicts the coronation of

Fig. 99
St Peter denies Christ,
from a light in Hardman's
south transept window
illustrating the life of
St Peter, 1871.

Fig. 100
St Michael, in C. E. Kempe's
north ambulatory window,
1881.

Henry III in the abbey in 1216 (fig. 97). Henry was crowned in Gloucester rather than London because of the parlous state in which his father, King John, had left the country, the capital being in the hands of the French. Either side of the boy and crowning him are the papal legate, Gualo, and the bishop of Winchester, Peter des Roches. The other window (from 1859) shows Abbot Thokey receiving into the abbey in 1327 the body of Edward II. In the tracery lights above are episodes associated with the king's imprisonment and death at Berkeley Castle. Below are shown his burial, the construction of the tomb and the arrival of pilgrims (see p. 26). In their two-dimensional character, fine drawing and rather 'hot' colours these windows are excellent examples of the best work of the period. They contrast with the much more muted palette of two slightly later Clayton & Bell windows in the north aisle; one is of the Nativity, and the other (designed by the young C. E. Kempe) depicts three men who were tortured by fire, among them Bishop Hooper.

The other windows in the nave were the work of the relatively local workshops of Joseph Bell (Bristol) and George Rogers (Worcester) and of the London workshops of William Warrington, Frederick Preedy and Ward & Hughes. Here, as everywhere else apart from the Lady Chapel and some clerestories, no record was made of the surviving medieval glass noted by Waller and others, and none of this was incorporated into the new work. It was possibly kept for repairs elsewhere or, in the case of more substantial fragments, sold to collectors; much, no doubt, was smashed.

The next phase of re-glazing filled the two large north (1876) and south (1871) windows in the transepts with Hardman glass, depicting the lives of St Paul (north) and St Peter (south; fig. 99). The west window of the south transept is a memorial by Clayton & Bell to Thomas Gambier Parry; the subjects include St Luke, traditionally a painter, and

Fra Angelico. The position is appropriate as the window is opposite St Andrew's Chapel where the walls and vault were painted in spirit fresco by Gambier Parry between 1866 and 1868 (fig. 98).

The final phase of Victorian work was the re-glazing of the quire ambulatories, between 1878 and 1892, by Charles Eamer Kempe. These six windows are typical of Kempe's earlier and probably better work. Although there is no common theme, the windows do have a stylistic unity. As a young man Kempe had been a close observer, especially with his sketchbook, of fifteenth-century glass; he was also influenced by William Morris and his circle. This all shows in features of the Gloucester glass: extensive use of silver (yellow) stain, often applied on blue glass to produce a distinctive sage green; intricate detail, especially of fabric and jewels; fine painting of facial features; and the use of peacock feathers in angel's wings, as, for example, in the striking figure of St Michael (fig. 100). In most cases, beneath each of the figures in the large main lights is a smaller, associated scene. For example, below Adam leaning nonchalantly on his spade, he and Eve stare intently at one another, each holding an apple. In another window, illustrating four events in the history of the abbey, Abbot Seabroke stands above a scene in which he admires the abbey's new tower.

J. L. Pearson's restoration of the Lady Chapel
Scott had appointed John Ashbee as his clerk of works. On Ashbee's resignation in 1872 F. S. Waller was reappointed supervisor of works, and on Scott's death in 1878 he became resident architect. Significant work was completed between 1878 and 1881 on the stonework of the tower, especially the pinnacles and parapet, but financial problems meant that little else was achieved (other than re-glazing), and in 1881 Waller suggested that his salary should be reduced, such was the paucity of work. Clergy and other cathedral employees soon had to follow his example. This situation was to change with the appointment in 1889 of J. W. Sheringham as archdeacon and residentiary canon. He took responsibility for an appeal for funds, especially for the restoration of the Lady Chapel, the one major area hitherto largely untouched. In six years some £9,000 was raised.

Although Waller in his report of 1855 had noted that the roof of the chapel was in a better condition than others in the cathedral, he had also recommended a significant programme of repair and restoration; external stonework, tiled floor and glazing, in particular, demanded attention, and, as almost everywhere in the cathedral, lime wash

needed to be removed. Scott had, in general, endorsed Waller's view, agreeing, as already noted, that the reredos should be left in its damaged state.

Little had been done, however, and the state of the building rapidly deteriorated. After 1873 services ceased to be held there, and writers described wind and rain driving in and glass falling out of the crumbling stonework of the windows. This was not a new situation. Gambier Parry, writing in 1883 in *Records of Gloucester Cathedral*, remembered being told of the floor being 'strewn with glass and stones' many years earlier, and of learning from another 'that the boys of the College School used to amuse themselves by smashing with stones the northern windows which bounded their play-ground'.

Urgent action was required, and the chapter asked J. L. Pearson, the architect of Truro Cathedral, for his advice. He reported in 1892 and again in 1895. By the latter date work had begun on the parapet, and in the next two years external stonework was repaired, the roof re-leaded, the interior cleaned of lime wash and the floor relaid, reusing the memorial ledgers and medieval tiles on a new concrete base.

The glass of Christopher Whall
The glazing of the very large windows of the Lady Chapel remained unresolved. In 1897 the chapter, influenced clearly by Dean Spence, decided to ask Christopher Whall to submit designs for the two smaller west windows of the chapel. On the basis of these he was commissioned to 're-glaze the windows of the Lady Chapel excluding the windows in the sanctuary'; this unfortunate exclusion was due to the fact that the chapter had already given permission for the window on the south side of the sanctuary to be glazed by Heaton, Butler & Bayne. The granting of this important commission to the relatively inexperienced Whall was a brave step. It is, however, worth noting that the chapter stated that funds were limited, and Whall's colleagues agreed unanimously

Fig. 101
The Virgin Mary greets her cousin Elizabeth, from a series in the Lady Chapel designed by Christopher Whall, 1902.

Fig. 102
The Adoration, Lady Chapel, 1901. Note the medieval glass in the head of the light, which was retained and used by Whall.

Fig. 103
St Etheldreda and St Swithun, Lady Chapel, 1902. The detail of Swithun's cope is typical of Whall's work.

to accept reduced wages in order to obtain such important work.

Whall was inspired by the ideas of the Arts and Crafts movement. In a reaction against the factory production methods of many of the leading manufacturers of stained glass he worked with a small team of men and women, sharing responsibilities and following the practice of a medieval workshop in completing all the stages of the making of a window.

Vibrant colours and painting of the highest quality typify Whall's work and illustrate his close supervision of his workshop. He exploited fully the

potential of the newly developed slab glass, with its thickness, rich colours and varied tones. Whall designed most of the figures, some of them drawn from life: for example, his wife modelled St Hilda and his daughter St Agnes. Throughout there is exquisite painting of detail, especially that drawn from nature: the organic canopies, the birds, animals and butterflies, and the leaves, berries and flowers, especially in the white quarries.

Whall was also sensitive to the buildings in which he worked. His advice was to 'be modest and reticent; know the styles of the past thoroughly and add your

Fig. 104
Christ enthroned, with the Virgin Mary and Mary Magdalene, by Christopher Whall, Lady Chapel, 1909.

of the entrance with the Fall, with Eve and the serpent in the Garden of Eden. Episodes from Mary's life follow in the centre of the next two windows on each side. On the left she is taught to read by her mother, Anne, and then across three lights the Annunciation is shown, with Mary kneeling as she receives Gabriel's message. Opposite, Mary visits her cousin Elizabeth to tell her the news of her pregnancy (fig. 101). Then the Adoration of the newborn Jesus by shepherds and magi is shown against a beautifully realised snowy landscape; above Mary medieval glass was retained as part of the shaft of light shining down on her and the Child (fig. 102). Finally, on the right by the entrance, the wheat and grapes stand for the reconciliation of God and the world through the death and Resurrection of Christ; humankind is represented by the kneeling and clothed Adam and Eve.

The glass in each of the four main windows has a common vertical theme. Reading from the top, there is: an archangel; a group of angels; one of the four episodes in Mary's life, with accompanying martyr-saints of the early Church; British saints; and scenes (in most) from the lives of those saints (fig. 103).

Whall also prepared designs for the two sanctuary windows. Unfortunately the one for the south window has never been realised; it proved too contentious to remove the existing glass, even though Edward VII, visiting in 1909, is said to have regretted the failure to complete the full scheme. However, to the left of the altar is Whall's interpretation of the reconciliation of man to God through the Incarnation (1909; fig. 104). Below the dramatically vivid blue and red angels sits Christ enthroned, with the crowned Virgin Mary and Eve on one side, and Mary Magdalene and Adam on the other. Under them are St John, St Paul, St Peter, St Andrew and St James, and in the lowest tier are scenes from the life of the Virgin.

In 1903 Whall filled the large chapter house

own fresh feeling to them reverently.' Thus he retained the medieval glass generally as it existed: canopies in the heads of many lights; faces, grotesques and symbols in small tracery lights; fragmentary detail in larger traceries. His understanding of medieval iconography is demonstrated in the attributes given to many of the saints.

The six windows of the original commission, installed between 1899 and 1902, are on a theme explained by Whall as 'the dignity to which human nature has been raised by the Incarnation of Christ through the Virgin Mary'. The series starts to the left

Fig. 105
Osric, founder of the Saxon
monastery, St Peter and
St Paul, in Christopher
Whall's chapter house
window, 1903.

Fig. 106
William the Conqueror, flanked by
Bishop Odo and Abbot Serlo,
ordering the compilation of the
Domesday survey, by Christopher
Whall, chapter house, 1903.

Fig. 105
Osric, founder of the Saxon monastery, St Peter and St Paul, in Christopher Whall's chapter house window, 1903.

Fig. 106
William the Conqueror, flanked by Bishop Odo and Abbot Serlo, ordering the compilation of the Domesday survey, by Christopher Whall, chapter house, 1903.

window with glass on the themes of Discipline, Counsel and Valour. The centre lights show (above) Osric, the founder of the Saxon monastery, with St Peter and St Paul (fig. 105) and (below) William the Conqueror ordering the (Domesday) survey of his kingdom (fig. 106).

In all of these windows there is much white glass and many subtle tints of grey, brown and green. Against these the rich colours of the slab glass, in Whall's word, 'sing'. The American architect Ralph Adams Cram described these 'extraordinary new windows' as 'at the same time perfectly medieval and perfectly modern'. Whall and his team had given to Gloucester what is generally seen as the finest stained glass of the Arts and Crafts movement.

The Arts and Crafts movement

Whall knew and worked with some of the leading members of the Arts and Crafts movement. For example, the architect J. D. Sedding, who had designed one of Kempe's ambulatory windows, gave him his first major commission. Henry Wilson, Sedding's assistant and successor, became a friend of Whall and was responsible for some important work in the cathedral. In 1898 he designed the memorial in the north aisle to Canon Douglas Tinling. In this strong, beautiful work, in marble, bronze and lapis lazuli, Tinling kneels and a child angel leads him to the entrance to the Holy City (fig. 108). Wilson also designed the memorial to Canon Evan Evans in the south transept. However, his most unusual work is the 'wildly cranky' clock in the north transept (fig. 107), installed in 1903 as a memorial to Canon Bartholomew Price, a Fellow of the Royal Astronomical Society. Signs of the zodiac represent the hours, although at the top are the Virgin and Child, and in the large centre roundel are two figures, possibly Love pushing back Death's (or Time's) spear.

Among other monuments contemporary with these are two worth noting: the small memorial

Fig. 107
The north transept clock face, designed by Henry Wilson, in memory of Canon Bartholomew Price, 1903.

tablet in the Lady Chapel to Dorothea Beale (1831–1906), principal of Cheltenham Ladies' College, with an inscription by Eric Gill (c.1907) and the large memorial (1909) in the south ambulatory to Dr Charles Ellicott, bishop of Gloucester from 1863 to 1905; this latter is distinctly not in the Arts and Crafts style.

In the Treasury are three important pieces from this period. Wilson's Tinling chalice (1900) is an elaborate work, with four blue-green rivers flowing from a lamb held in the central knop; the foot has seven domes, seven trees and seven towers, set with fire opals (fig. 109). Sedding's flagon (1891) shows the pelican feeding her young with her own blood. Much more simple but equally beautiful is C. R. Ashbee's chalice of 1903, made at the Guild of Handicraft at Chipping Campden.

Also made at the Guild, between 1903 and 1905, were the beaten copper panels on the east wall of the chapter house, recording the Gloucestershire dead of the Boer War. Whall provided examples of the lettering he was using in his glass, so that the coppersmiths could copy it. The memorial and Whall's window above it recorded the past. However, the list of dead of the former and the emphasis on the qualities of discipline and valour in the latter point, unconsciously, to the coming war.

In a little over half a century the seemingly little-cared-for Georgian cathedral had been transformed. The remarkably sympathetic conservation, restoration and refurnishing had been generally completed in a manner that harmonised with the medieval building. Waller in 1855 had stated that the intention was 'to more thoroughly adapt it to the requirements of the present day'. By 1914 that had been largely achieved artistically, architecturally and liturgically.

Robin Lunn

Fig. 108
The north aisle
memorial to Canon
Douglas Tinling,
designed by Henry
Wilson, 1898.

Fig. 109
Henry Wilson's chalice,
held in the Treasury,
given in memory of
Canon Douglas Tinling,
1900.

INHABITING THE SPACE

THE VICTORIAN REORDERING at Gloucester Cathedral preserved, as it did in so many other places, the fabric of the church, enhancing its worshipping life and ensuring its survival into the present. It has to be said, however, that some of the Victorians' building materials and practices have caused problems for their successors. Corrosion of soft stone and the use of iron bars have necessitated extensive repairs to some parts of the cathedral.

Restoration and conservation

The outbreak of the First World War in 1914 saw an end to any major work on the cathedral for some time. F. W. Waller, who had succeeded his father as architect in 1905, had overseen the restoration and strengthening of the tower from 1907 until 1911. He also installed electric light in the nave (1911) and quire (1914). The ugly gas pipes were removed, the pillars were made good, and the whole nave vault was cleaned and renovated where necessary. The thought of those who lit the gas lights climbing up into the triforium and leaning out to ignite the jets is one to make present-day health and safety committees shudder.

The period immediately after the war was one of only two in the cathedral's history when it did not employ its own stonemasons (the other was during the Civil War). Colonel Waller, the third-generation architect, started up a team again in the 1930s, when urgent repairs were needed to the stonework around many of the windows in the quire, the south transept, the Lady Chapel and the nave. When war broke out again in 1939, the crypt pillars were strengthened in case the cathedral was bombed. The effigy of Duke Robert of Normandy was taken down to the crypt for safety, and a mysterious package arrived from Westminster Abbey for storage. This subsequently proved to be the Coronation Chair, incorporating the Stone of Scone. Cathedral guides like to tell people that this was the closest that Duke Robert ever got to

the English throne. Evidence of wartime precautions can still be seen in the small holes in the cloister vaulting. These were to provide an escape route for the water, should the fire hoses ever be called into action.

Colonel Waller had been concerned about the state of the cathedral roofs during the 1930s, but it was not until 1952 that a major appeal was launched to fund their restoration. It was a twenty-year project, during which some of the outer stonework of the cathedral was cleaned. The grime of centuries was washed off, revealing the golden stone underneath. This work continued on the south side throughout the 1980s. More roof work had to be undertaken in the 1970s and 1980s. Although Waller had retired in 1960, the architects who oversaw this work, Bernard Ashwell and later Basil Comely, were from the same firm.

The 900th anniversary of the laying of the foundation stone of the Norman abbey by Abbot Serlo was celebrated in 1989. Under the patronage of HRH The Prince of Wales the 900 Year Fund was set up, with the aim of raising £4 million for restoration and conservation of the fabric. One of the most exciting projects was the reordering of the south ambulatory chapel and, with the help of the Sylvanus Lysons Trust, the commissioning of new stained glass for its windows (fig. 110). This was one of Tom Denny's earliest works and is greatly loved. The left and right windows are based on Psalm 148, in which all creation praises God. The central window shows the figure of the disciple Thomas kneeling before the risen Christ, who reconciles earth and heaven in a new creation. The more these windows are contemplated, the more there is to be seen; as the daylight and the seasons vary, different details are brought into focus. Another of the 900th-anniversary commissions was the set of six festal copes that the cathedral clergy wear at Christmas, Easter and Pentecost and other great festivals. These

Fig. 110
The stained glass of the south ambulatory chapel, created by Tom Denny in 1993.

were created by Belinda Scarlett in different coloured silks. New frontals for the high altar, too, were commissioned from Alice Kettle.

In preparation for the coming anniversary the clerks of the works, Tom Dorrington in the 1970s and Alan Norton in the 1980s had built up a strong team of stonemasons. In 1990 Pascal Mychalysin arrived from France to join them. Pascal became Master Mason in 1996. Much work was done on the tower, the south porch and the Lady Chapel, then the west end, the north aisle roof and the quire parapets. Perhaps the most easily visible new stonework is that of the *lavatorium*, begun in 1997 and completed in 2002, with its fine details of animal and human heads. The masons also worked on the restoration of the Great East Window in 2000, replacing some of the tracery with new stone. The south aisle (fig. 111) has been a long-term project, interrupted by the need for urgent work on the east turrets of the north and south transepts. Ten new gargoyles (fig. 112), funded by generous patrons, were carved to carry the rainwater well away from the building, replacing Victorian gargoyles that had ceased to do their job. Many new ballflowers were created around the outside of the windows to replace or match those of the medieval masons.

In general, the cathedral is probably in a better condition than at any time since the Reformation,

but it is a constant challenge to raise the funds to restore, conserve and maintain the building. Another important consideration is the need to pass on skills to the next generation, and in 2006 the cathedral's Stonemasons Fellowship was inaugurated; this is now a foundation degree course in partnership with the University of Gloucestershire.

After twenty years repairing and renewing the stonework of his medieval and Victorian forebears, Pascal Mychalysin is still bowled over by the cathedral:

The miracle of Gloucester is that it is an improbable building. In stylistic terms it should not exist, because of its two entirely different parts. It is a marvellous example of human ingenuity and intellectual freedom. The medieval craftsmen were not afraid to use different parts together and were not constrained by the conventional, combining ingenuity with efficiency. A lot of what they did in the quire is a marvel of design and also a very efficient way of maximising resources. This is the first perpendicular building and it is still stunning. It is a work of genius.

Many of the cathedral's visitors, as well as those who live within sight of the tower rising above the skyline and those who inhabit the space day by day, would agree with him.

Fig. 113
The First World War memorial window tells of the heavy loss of life borne by the Gloucestershire Regiment.

Fig. 114
All who died in the loss of HMS *Gloucester* off Crete in May 1941 are remembered here.

War and peace

One of the spaces in the cathedral most valued by local people and visitors is the Memorial Chapel in the north ambulatory. Here the memorials to the dead of the First and Second World Wars and the Korean War bring home the scale of the loss of life borne by the people of Gloucestershire in the twentieth century.

Men from the Gloucestershire Regiment, which traces its history back to 1694, served in many of the fiercest battles of the First World War, in France, Flanders (Belgium) and Italy and also in Gallipoli, Mesopotamia (Iraq), Persia (Iran) and Macedonia. Seventy-two new battle honours were secured for the Regiment, but 8,100 Gloucesters (or Glosters, as they are often known) were killed (fig. 113). Among the dead was the poet Cyril Winterbotham. His fellow Gloucestershire poets W. F. Harvey and Ivor Gurney survived the war, but with their physical and mental health broken. Both are remembered in the cathedral. Gurney was also a composer, and his memorial is near the door to the organ loft.

The Royal Gloucester Hussars have a memorial to their fallen in College Green. During the First World War they served at Gallipoli and in Egypt and Palestine, and in the Second they played a crucial part in the North African campaign. They fought in several battles before they were disbanded after the Battle of Alam el Halfa in 1942.

During the Second World War men from the Glosters were among the first to land in France in 1939, and they defended the approaches to Dunkirk in 1940 while tens of thousands of troops were evacuated. Several hundred were taken prisoner as a consequence. Others were back in France in June 1944, taking part in the D-Day landings in Normandy. The 1st Glosters fought in Burma from 1941 until 1942, and the 10th were trained for jungle warfare in India before taking part in the Burma campaign of 1944–45. During the six years

Fig. 115
The Celtic cross carved by Colonel Carne while in captivity during the Korean War.

Fig. 116
This window commemorates those who died at Imjin River in 1951 and all who served in the Korean War.

of war 870 men were killed. The name of each individual who died on active service during the two world wars is beautifully inscribed in the relevant memorial book in the chapel. The King's School has its own inscribed tablet in the Lady Chapel. We can only imagine the collective grief of those left behind when so many husbands, sons and brothers were killed.

The Royal Navy lost over 2,000 men in the evacuation of Allied forces after the German invasion of Crete. Their sacrifice allowed 15,000 troops to be saved and taken to North Africa. On the east side of the chapel, the window by Edward Payne remembers the 723 men who died when HMS *Gloucester* was sunk off Crete on 22 May 1941 (fig. 114).

Only five years after the end of the Second World War the men of the Glosters were called to active service again in the Korean War of 1950–53. In 1945, at the onset of the Cold War, Korea had been partitioned; the Russians and Chinese backed a Stalinist regime in North Korea, while the United Nations supported the administration in South Korea. The men of the Glosters were truly heroic in their attempt to block the Chinese route to Seoul at the Battle of Imjin River in April 1951, for which they were awarded the unique American Citation by

President Truman. Losses were heavy, and the west window of the chapel, by Alan Younger, commemorates these (fig. 116). Many others were taken prisoner and endured great hardship at the hands of their Korean and Chinese captors. One of the greatest treasures of the cathedral is a small Celtic cross carved with two nails and a rudimentary hammer by Colonel Carne during his imprisonment in Korea (fig. 115). It was placed on a makeshift altar for a celebration of Holy Communion at Christmas 1951 and provided a symbol of hope and endurance for the prisoners of war so far from home. The cross was presented to the dean and chapter when Colonel Carne returned home in 1953.

Since the Korean War ended, the Glosters have been on active service in Cyprus, Northern Ireland, Bosnia, Iraq and Afghanistan. In 1994, after 300 years, the Glosters were amalgamated with the Duke of Edinburgh's Royal Regiment to form the Royal Gloucestershire, Berkshire and Wiltshire Regiment. The RGBW was amalgamated with several other regiments in 2007 to form The Rifles, but the famous 'back badge', issued in memory of the Battle of Alexandria in 1801, still remains a part of their history and is worn by the 1st Battalion The Rifles. Every two years a service is held in the cathedral for

the regiment as close to Back Badge Day, 21 March, as possible.

The war in Iraq and the fighting in Afghanistan have inflicted many casualties on The Rifles. Those on active service, the wounded and the dead are remembered in the prayers of the cathedral. In 2007 a new sculpture by Rory Young was commissioned for the Memorial Chapel, to fill a niche above the altar that had been empty since the Reformation (fig. 117). The subject was chosen for its significance to the armed forces: Jesus hangs on the cross between the two criminals, while the Roman centurion traditionally known as Longinus looks on. It was this soldier who said when Jesus died, 'Truly, this man was the Son of God'.

The cathedral and the city maintain links with the present-day HMS *Gloucester*, the tenth ship of her name to serve in the Royal Navy. Together with the Glosters, the ship's company have the freedom of the city, and special services are sometimes held in the cathedral before and after spells of duty overseas. Gloucestershire is proud of those who serve in the armed forces of the Crown, and the cathedral is a place where their dedication and commitment can be honoured.

Music and musicians

Gloucester Cathedral has always been proud of its musical heritage and the contribution made by its organists and singers to the Anglican choral tradition. Apart from the years of the Civil War and the Commonwealth in the seventeenth century, musicians have been employed by the chapter to provide choral services from 1541 to the present day. The line of organists can be traced back from the appointment of Adrian Partington as Director of Music in 2008 to Robert Lichfield in 1576. The south chantry of the Lady Chapel, often known as the Musicians' Chapel, commemorates many of the organists and composers most closely associated

Fig. 117
A new sculpture, showing the crucifixion of Jesus with the Roman centurion looking on, 2007.

with the cathedral in the nineteenth and twentieth centuries: S. S. Wesley, Herbert Brewer, Herbert Sumsion, Herbert Howells and John Sanders.

The cathedral choir sings the setting of the Mass at the Sunday Eucharist (each week in term time) and Evensong (Sunday, Tuesday, Wednesday, Friday and Saturday). Lay clerks and choral scholars provide the men's voices, while the treble line is served by boy choristers from the King's School. This has been the case since the school's foundation in 1541. It is a heavy workload for all the musicians. A chorister's day is a very busy one. An early morning rehearsal in the Song School, which has been occupied by

countless generations of choristers, is followed by a normal school day. After their lessons, when most of their fellow pupils have gone home, choristers return to the cathedral for another rehearsal before singing Evensong. It is an exciting and a challenging life, providing a first-class musical education. Many former choristers have gone on to a career in some form of music-making.

The cathedral's youth choir (fig. 118) was founded in 2000, to give other young people the opportunity of singing in the cathedral. Girls and boys aged between thirteen and nineteen from all over the county are welcome to audition for the youth choir, which plays an important part in the musical life of the cathedral. The youth choir sings Evensong every Thursday. They also sing at some of the Christmas and Easter services and on other occasions in the Church's year. One former chorister and youth choir member, who as an adult has sung in three other cathedral choirs, has said: 'The choral and musical education I have received in my time at Gloucester Cathedral has been amazing. Being a chorister and then member of the youth choir – with the additional experiences of things like the Royal Maundy Service, several Three Choirs Festivals and choir tours abroad – is something I will never forget. It provided the opportunity to meet and work with musicians of outstanding ability.'

One of the most important dimensions of the cathedral's musical life is the Three Choirs Festival (figs 119 and 121). Each Director of Music at Gloucester, Hereford and Worcester is the principal conductor when the festival is hosted by their cathedral, and the responsibility of choosing the music to be performed is theirs. In addition to the sung services, the cathedral becomes a concert hall for the nine days of the festival, combining performances of English choral and orchestral works with a wider repertoire. The festival continues its commitment to commissioning new music. In recent years compositions by James MacMillan, John McCabe and John Joubert have been premiered.

The twentieth-century English composers most associated with the Three Choirs Festival are Elgar, Vaughan Williams, Finzi and Howells. Herbert Howells had been a chorister at Gloucester Cathedral. In 1910 he attended the premier of Vaughan Williams's *Fantasia on a Theme of Thomas Tallis*, conducted by the composer. This was thought to be 'strange and incomprehensible' by the audience at the time. It was followed by the first complete performance in Gloucester of Elgar's *The Dream of Gerontius*. Howells wrote afterwards:

He (RVW) left the rostrum … and came to the empty chair next to mine, carrying a copy of *Gerontius*, and presently was sharing it with me, while Elgar was conducting the first hearing I ever had of the *Dream*. For a music-bewildered youth of seventeen it was an overwhelming evening, so disturbing and moving that I even asked RVW for his autograph – and got it! … And I still have what I now know to be a

Fig. 119
The opening service of the Three Choirs Festival, with the cathedral choir and the festival chorus.

Fig. 120
John Sanders, organist 1967–94 and composer, was artistic director of many Festivals.

Fig. 121
Fringe events attract the crowds at the Three Choirs Festival before and after concerts.

supreme commentary by one great composer upon another – the *Fantasia on a Theme by Thomas Tallis*.' (quoted in Anthony Boden's *Three Choirs: A History of the Festival*)

Elgar had strong links with the three cities of Hereford, Worcester and Gloucester. Between the two world wars he became an integral part of the Three Choirs Festival. As well as being seen on the conductor's rostrum at performances of his own works, he could often be met socialising with members of the audience in the company of his great friend George Bernard Shaw. While his music was generally neglected elsewhere in the country, it remained in the festival's repertoire. Performances of

The Apostles, The Kingdom and *Gerontius* drew larger audiences even than those for the staples of Mendelssohn's *Elijah* and Handel's *Messiah*.

Elgar died in 1934, and the festival at Gloucester that year was a sad one. Holst and Delius had also died, and Vaughan Williams was unable to attend. Three years later Vaughan Williams's *Dona Nobis Pacem* was the main new work of the festival. It was a cry for peace from someone who had experienced the horrors of the First World War. On the very day that the festival was due to open in Hereford in 1939 war was declared, and it was to be seven years before the Three Choirs Festival could resume. The great new work of 1946 was Gerald Finzi's *Dies Natalis*, described at its first performance as 'inexpressibly

rare and delightful and beautiful'. In 1950 Finzi's *Intimations of Immortality* was premiered, as was the *Hymnus Paradisi* by Howells. The Gloucester festival of 1956 was Vaughan Williams's last, at which he conducted *The Lark Ascending*, for solo violin and orchestra, now one of the best-loved works of the twentieth century. The whole cathedral rose to honour him. 'As the great man took his place on the rostrum both audience and choir rose to their feet in tribute. They stood again at the end.'

The works of these composers are still an integral part of the repertoire of the world's oldest music festival and draw new generations of people to listen to and participate in their performance. Festival week is an exciting and vibrant time, as visitors from all over the world come to hear these and newer works, often written especially for the glorious performance space that is Gloucester Cathedral.

The most recent memorial in the Musicians' Chapel commemorates John Sanders, organist from 1967 until 1994 (fig. 120), whose compositions are receiving growing recognition. The memorial is a painting of the Annunciation to the Shepherds by the Gloucester-born Iain McKillop, who also painted the three panels in the Lady Chapel reredos (fig. 122). Here the angel choir and orchestra proclaim the good news of the birth of Christ. In the background can be seen the Gloucester valley, viewed from Birdlip Hill, including the cathedral and May Hill, favourite spots in the county.

Close by, Fiona Brown, in her memorial window for the organist and composer Herbert Sumsion, also depicted the landscape of the Slad valley so dear to him. Creating new works for ancient buildings can pose problems, as Caroline Swash found when working on the Howells window (fig. 123), also in

Fig. 122
Paintings of the crucifixion, pieta and resurrection of Jesus fill the broken niches of the Lady Chapel.

Fig. 123
The Howells memorial window shows snippetts of his compositions most associated with Gloucester.

the Musicians' Chapel but in a very different style from its other stained glass. She wrote: 'There will always be a battle in the creation of a truly contemporary work within a famous and much loved historic building which compromises neither the charm of the architecture nor the vision of the artist.'

Gathering communities

Music is one of the ways in which the cathedral gathers different communities into its life. Concerts are given several times a year by 'home' groups such as the Gloucester Choral Society and the St Cecilia Singers, and many other varied musical events involving large numbers of people are hosted by the cathedral. It also provides space for exhibitions of contemporary art, such as Antony Gormley's *Field for the British Isles* (2004) and the sculpture exhibition 'Crucible' (2010; fig. 124) as well as many smaller-scale displays of community art.

However, the cathedral is more than a venue for concerts and exhibitions. Principally, it is the seat (*cathedra*) of the bishop of Gloucester and the mother church of the diocese. As such, it is the gathering place of the clergy and people of the

Fig. 124
Seated Queen by Ralph
Brown and the distant
Kneeling Figure by Lyn
Chadwick, from the
exhibition 'Crucible',
2010.

diocese of Gloucester. At services of baptism and confirmation people of all ages and backgrounds come to make their public commitment to Christ. Ordinations of deacons and priests are held every year, as men and women offer themselves to serve in the ordained ministry in parishes throughout the diocese. The ministry of lay people is affirmed here too, in the annual services for readers and local ministry teams, and clergy and lay people together gather on Maundy Thursday to renew their commitment to the Christian life. At the great festivals of Christmas, Easter and Pentecost the bishop comes to his cathedral and preaches to the community of faith (fig. 125).

Cathedrals are places of national significance and also have a specific role in the life of the county. The monarch is represented by the Lord Lieutenant of Gloucestershire at several services and events in the cathedral every year. During Harvest Festival farmers' representatives from across the county bring examples of their produce to be blessed and given away. Awards ceremonies are held here for the county council, the University of Gloucestershire, the University of the West of England and Gloucestershire College. Throughout the year there are special services for many local organisations that want to celebrate their work in the cathedral.

The mayor of Gloucester is a frequent visitor to the cathedral during his or her year of office, especially in the Christmas season, when there are charity events almost every evening. Links with the city council are an important dimension to the life of the cathedral and the ministry of the city centre, both for those who live in Gloucester and for those who come to visit its cathedral. The cathedral is an icon for the city, and its many visitors contribute to the local economy.

It was really only in the 1970s that cathedrals began to experience tourism as it is understood today. At Gloucester visitor numbers rose dramatically, and volunteers were recruited to welcome visitors and guide them around the building. At first these volunteers were all members of the Friends of Gloucester Cathedral, an organisation founded in 1936 to help preserve the fabric of the cathedral and to support its religious and musical standards. The Friends still flourish and contribute a great deal to the life of the cathedral.

The pool of volunteers who play a part in the cathedral's ministry of welcome to visitors has widened since those early days. Well over 400 people are involved in volunteering. In addition to those encountered by visitors – welcomers, guides, tower tour guides, exhibition desk attendants, honorary chaplains, shop and coffee shop volunteers or flower arrangers – there are other groups who are busy behind the scenes. The monuments are kept spick and span by volunteers, who often grow very attached to the memorials they clean, and the choir, altar and clergy linen and vestments are washed, ironed and mended with great care. Stewards and servers are more visible as part of the cathedral's Sunday worship. As one person put it: 'volunteers see it as a great privilege to be part of the life of the cathedral, especially in the continuing care and welcome of all visitors.'

One group of people often heard but never seen are the bell-ringers. Every Sunday afternoon and Tuesday evening the bells are rung by a dedicated group of change-ringers, and the sound they make is heard all over the city. Gloucester has a peal of twelve bells; ten were re-hung in 1979, when two new bells were added. Once or twice a year, on bank holidays, a peal is rung, taking nearly four hours. Visitors who take the tower tour are able to see the bells, but no one can be in the belfry while they are being rung. However, the medieval bourdon bell, Great Peter, can be seen and heard striking the hour on the level of the bell chamber.

Sometimes visitors are surprised to see groups of

Fig. 125
The Bishop of Gloucester, The Right Revd Michael Perham, holding the historic diocesan staff.

small black-clad monks (fig. 126), colourful medieval pilgrims or a cross-section of Tudor society processing into and around the cathedral. These are children from Gloucestershire schools who have come to experience the living history that the building can offer. The Education Centre links the tours and activities it offers to the school curriculum, so the children can engage more deeply with a topic. They learn about the life of St Peter's Abbey and experience something of the continuing tradition of daily prayer and worship in the building today. Special trails are offered around the great festivals, helping all visiting children to appreciate the spirituality of the Christian story.

One school community that gathers in the cathedral day by day for assemblies or special services is the King's School, which is part of the Cathedral Foundation. Many former pupils enjoy returning to visit a building that they may not have fully appreciated first thing on a Monday morning in their school days.

The Benedictine tradition of hospitality continues through the provision of a coffee shop, where people can meet and greet one another. Once a week this space is used by volunteers to provide breakfast for the homeless of the city. It aims to be a safe and welcoming environment for people whose lives are sometimes chaotic or unfortunate in the changing circumstances of our times.

There are many different communities of people who come together in or around the cathedral, whether it is once a year for a special service or on a daily basis, like the staff who work in the office, shop and coffee shop, the masons and maintenance team who care for the fabric, and the vergers who are first in and last out of the building at the beginning and end of the day. All value their connection with the cathedral and give of their time, gifts and talents to enhance its ministry and mission in the local community.

Fig. 126
Children from a local school dress up to learn about life as a Benedictine monk.

Fig. 127
Candles are lit here every day by people of all ages and stages in life.

A house of prayer

As well as the communities who gather in the cathedral there are those individuals who slip in and out anonymously, day by day, week by week, to say a prayer, light a candle or simply sit and enjoy the space in peace (fig. 127). This is the fundamental purpose of the cathedral: to be a house of prayer, a sacred space into which people can enter as deeply or as peripherally as they wish. Seven days a week, 365 days a year, it is open for anyone who wishes to come in.

The cathedral was built for the worship of God, and it has served this fundamental purpose throughout the centuries. Today, each and every day there is a service of Holy Communion, Morning Prayer is said, and Evening Prayer is either said or sung. Archbishop Cranmer, in the first Prayer Book of 1549, created these two daily services out of the former eight offices of monastic worship which would have been sung by the monks of St Peter's Abbey.

As it was in monastic times, the worshipping heart of the cathedral during the week is the quire, where Evensong is sung and clergy and congregation gather to pray. The side-chapels are used for daily

Fig. 128
Choir, congregation and
clergy gather round the
nave altar to celebrate the
Eucharist on Sundays.

Fig. 129
Sunlight pours through
the windows of the nave
clerestory, adding awe and
mystery to the worship.

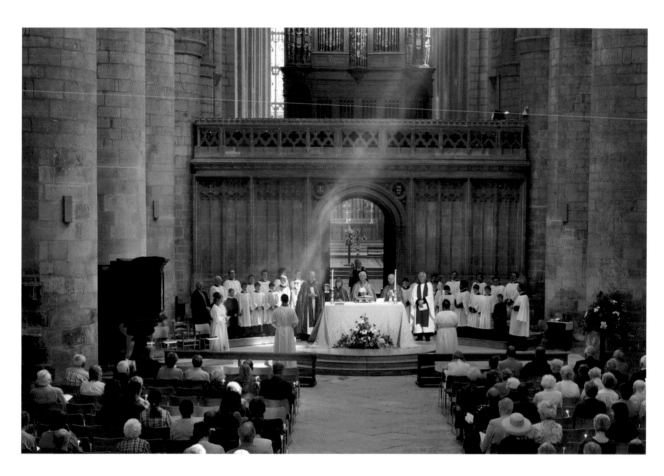

Communion and Morning Prayer, giving an intimacy to the worship and a variety of space, both of which are greatly valued. On Sundays the focus moves to the nave for the Sung Eucharist as the worshipping community gathers to hear the words of scripture and to receive the bread and wine, symbols of Christ's body and blood given for the world (fig. 128). Those who are present participate by coming together in communion with God and with one another, in order that they may go out into the world over the week ahead to reflect God's love in Christ.

It is the quality and the continuity of the daily worship that give the cathedral its special atmosphere as a place of prayer and that encourage the prayers of visitors (fig. 129). An important daily task of the canon-in-residence on duty is to gather up the prayers left on the prayer desk and offer them in worship. Through these prayers there is a connection between the cathedral and the concerns of countless people who seek solace in this safe and holy place. Some come back on another occasion and give thanks for prayers answered or lives turned around. In a fast-changing world the cathedral can be a symbol of stability and rootedness for many people with a variety of needs.

Perhaps it is at Evensong that continuity and change are juxtaposed and intertwined most closely (fig. 130). Most of the words used are those of the Book of Common Prayer, unchanged for centuries, but the Bible readings and the prayers are in modern English. The choral settings vary from those of the great Tudor composers Tallis, Byrd and Gibbons to

those of present-day composers such as John Tavener
and Jonathan Dove, with music from every century
in between. Works by S. S. Wesley, Brewer, Sumsion,
Howells and Sanders are part of the repertoire week
by week, reminding us of the contribution made by
Gloucester's musicians to the Anglican choral
tradition. Those who come to Evensong never cease
to be amazed at how the stresses of the day can be
washed away in music and prayer, and how
something of the eternal changelessness of God can
be experienced. The great space of the quire is filled
with sound and with silence, worship in the here and
now rising to the vault, where the angel choir
surround and worship the risen Christ in a depiction
of heaven.

From the moment of entry into the cathedral this
is the intended effect. Everyone who steps over the
threshold is invited to share in this glimpse of heaven
through the building itself and the prayers of those
who inhabit it. It is perhaps easier to experience this
when the nave is empty of chairs. The eye can absorb
the space and then be drawn beyond the solid
Norman pillars of the nave, through the quire to the
Great East Window. Sometimes the sun shining
through the windows of the south aisle gives a
jewelled effect on the floor and pillars, a glimpse of

Fig. 131
Stone, glass and light lend majesty to the building as a visiting choir prepares to lead Evensong.

glory to gladden the heart. Changes of light during a single day and during the seasons of the year can bring different aspects of the cathedral into focus.

The life of the cathedral has its own rhythm each day, each week, each year, as the festivals of the Church are celebrated. After a great service, perhaps a Christmas carol service at which there have been over a thousand people singing praise to God, when everyone has left the building and all is quiet, there is a sense of the cathedral settling back into itself, absorbing the effects of music and prayer into its very stones, adding to the layers of holiness left by former generations (fig. 131). Those who have most to do

with the cathedral are aware that they are but its temporary stewards and recipients of God's grace through it. We pass through its enduring life fleetingly on our brief human journey.

Like many who have gone before, perhaps, those who love Gloucester Cathedral may wish to say with Jacob, who dreamed of angels ascending and descending a ladder between earth and heaven and of God's promise to be with him: 'How awesome is this place! This is none other than the house of God, and this is the gate of heaven' (Genesis 28:17).

CELIA THOMSON

FURTHER READING

The following books may be obtained by the general reader through bookshops or the public library network. In addition to these, a more detailed list of relevant printed works, including journal articles, has been supplied by the authors of individual chapters. This will be found in the library section of the Gloucester Cathedral website, www.gloucestercathedral.org.uk.

General

Boden, A., *Three Choirs: A History of the Festival* (Alan Sutton, 1992)

Herbert, N. M. (ed.), *Victoria County History*, IV: *The City of Gloucester* (OUP, 1988)

Moss, P., *Historic Gloucester: An Illustrated Guide to the City and its Buildings* (Nonsuch, 2005)

Oxford Dictionary of National Biography (OUP, 2004; online edn, 2008)

Verey, D., and Brooks, A., *The Buildings of England: Gloucestershire, 2: The Vale and the Forest of Dean* (Yale University Press, 2002)

Welander, D., *The Stained Glass of Gloucester Cathedral* (Gloucester Cathedral, 1985)

Welander, D., *The History, Art and Architecture of Gloucester Cathedral* (Alan Sutton, 1991)

Abbot Serlo and the Norman abbey

Thurlby, M., *Romanesque Gloucestershire: Architecture, Sculpture and Painting* (Logaston Press, forthcoming)

Edward II and the abbey transformed

Alexander, J., and Binski, P. (eds), *Age of Chivalry: Art in Plantagenet England, 1200–1400* (Weidenfeld and Nicolson, 1987)

Haines, R. M., *King Edward II* (McGill-Queen's University Press, 2003)

Luxford, J. M., *The Art and Architecture of English Benedictine Monasteries, 1300–1540: A Patronage History* (Boydell Press, 2005)

Marks, R., *Image and Devotion in Late Medieval Britain* (Sutton Publishing, 2004)

Wilson, C., *The Gothic Cathedral* (Thames and Hudson, 1990)

Reformation and Civil War

Duffy, E., *The Stripping of the Altars: Traditional Religion in England, 1400–1580* (Yale University Press, 1992)

Duffy, E., *Voices of Morebath: Reformation and Rebellion in an English Village* (Yale University Press, 2001)

Fincham, K., and Tyacke, N., *Altars Restored: The Changing Face of English Religious Worship 1547–c.1700* (OUP, 2007)

MacCulloch, D., *The Later Reformation in England, 1547–1603* (Macmillan, 1990)

Cathedral and community

Bell, A., *Cathedral: Reflections in Gloucester Cathedral* (Arthur Bell, 1988)

Kemp, B., *English Church Monuments* (Batsford, 1980)

The Victorian reordering

Cormack, P., *The Stained Glass Work of Christopher Whall, 1849–1924* (Boston, 1999)

Harrison, M., *Victorian Stained Glass* (Barrie & Jenkins, 1980)

Hill, R., *God's Architect: Pugin and the Building of Romantic Britain* (Allen Lane, 2007)

Manton, C., *Henry Wilson, Practical Idealist* (Lutterworth Press, 2009)

Stavridi, M., *Master of Glass: Charles Eamer Kempe, 1837–1907* (The Kempe Society, 1988)

Victoria and Albert Museum, *Victorian Church Art* (London, 1971)

Inhabiting the space

The Benedictine Handbook (Canterbury Press, 2003)

Scott, D., *Cap of Honour; The Story of the Gloucestershire Regiment (the 28th/61st Foot), 1694–1950* (Sutton Publishing, 2005)

INDEX

Page numbers in *italics* are for illustrations

ACKNOWLEDGEMENTS

The Chapter of Gloucester Cathedral are extremely grateful to the authors of this book for giving so much of their time to the project; to the cathedral archivist, Chris Jeens, for all his help in sourcing pictures and commenting on the text; to all those who gave permission to use their photographs – Margaret Brown (fig. 112), Richard Cann (figs 76, 94–97 and 99–106), Derek Foxton (figs 119 and 121), John Jones (figs 30–35, 88 and 131 © www.skycell.net), Steve Russell (fig. 124) and Neil Wildin (front cover); and to Marion Farley for permission to use the photo of the Edward II window (fig. 20) and the portrait of John Sanders (fig. 120) by her late husband, Jack Farley. Thanks are also due to Gloucestershire Archives for their help with documents and photography and to Angelo Hornak for his photography and gracious goodwill.

The authors are grateful to those who read and commented on their text and for the improvements they suggested, and the Chapter also wish to thank the Friends of Gloucester Cathedral for their financial support for the book as part of their seventy-fifth anniversary celebrations.

Photography © Chapter of Gloucester Cathedral, 2011, except for the following: fig. 19 © The British Library Board (Royal 13 A. III, f.41v), 2011; fig. 50 © Castle Howard, North Yorkshire, UK/ The Bridgeman Art Library, 2011; figs 3 and 27 © Gloucestershire Archives (NF4-32GS p.4), 2011; figs 67, 74 and 75 © Gloucestershire Archives (B154-5041 Plates 9, 1 and 7), 2011; fig. 86 © Gloucestershire Archives (SR prints GL103-1GS), 2011; fig. 1 © Musee Marmottan, Paris, France/ Giraudon/The Bridgeman Art Library, 2011; fig.15 © The National Archives of the United Kingdom (C 150/1, f.18r), 2011; fig. 60 © Prado, Madrid, Spain/Giraudon/The Bridgeman Art Library, 2011; fig.16 © The Master and Fellows of St John's College Cambridge (MS A 7, f.1r), 2011; pp. 4 and 6, and figs 38, 43, 61, 87, 92, 111 and 122 © Marina Spironetti, 2011; and fig. 12 © Victoria and Albert Museum (No. 7649-1861), 2011.

First published in 2011 by
Scala Publishers Ltd
Northburgh House
10 Northburgh Street
London EC1V 0AT, UK
Telephone: +44 (0) 20 7 490 9900
www.scalapublishers.com

ISBN: 978 1 85759 667 0

All photographs are by Angelo Hornak, except for those listed above
Project managed by Esme West
Design by Nigel Soper
Plan by Gemma Bryant (Past Historic)

Printed and bound in China

10 9 8 7 6 5 4 3 2 1

Front Cover
The tower of Gloucester Cathedral is a landmark for many miles around.

Back Cover
The empty nave, as it would have been in the Middle Ages, is a glorious sacred space.

Title Page
The west walk of the cloisters showing the Morris & Co. stained-glass window.

Contents Page
Detail of the Madonna and Child from the window at the west end of the cloisters, 1924.

Foreword
The fourteenth-century angel vault of the quire, painted and gilded in the nineteenth century.